Walk like Jesus Walked

Volume 3

Making

Disciples

Fulfilling the Great Commission in Your Lifetime

Loren VanGalder

Spiritual Father Publications

ISBN-13: 978-1-7336556-7-5

Contents

Introduction

By this we may be sure that we are in him: whoever says, "I abide in him," ought to walk just as he walked (1 John 2:5–6).

A re you in Christ? Are you abiding in him? Are you walking like he walked?

Our goal in this series is to be Christ's presence in the world. In the first volume, we learned the foundation of that walk, and in the second, the culture of the kingdom. What's next? Jesus made it very clear in his Great Commission:

Then Jesus came to them and said, "All authority in heaven and on earth has been given to me. Therefore go and make disciples of all nations, baptizing them in the name of the Father and of the Son and of the Holy Spirit, and teaching them to obey everything I have commanded you. And surely I am with you always, to the very end of the age" (Matt. 28:18–20).

Was that command only for those apostles, or for every Christian? Jesus says that the task of making disciples would last until he returns. We will see that it is his call to every believer. Through the centuries, there has been much talk about completing the Great Commission. It should be the longing of every believer. Could we do that in your lifetime? I think it is possible. Never before have we had so many resources at our disposal.

What do you think of this proposition?

The only reason Jesus is delaying his return to this earth to establish his kingdom is the need to fulfill this commission and offer salvation to every nation.

God does not enjoy seeing wars, hunger, and suffering. He is not pleased with the ever-more-perverse sin or the lives and churches destroyed by Satan. For two millennia, he has been chafing to bind Satan and cast him and his demons into hell. Peter said in 2 Peter 3:9: *The Lord is not slow in keeping his promise, as some understand slowness. Instead he is patient with you, not wanting anyone to perish, but everyone to come to repentance.* And Jesus said in Matthew 24:14: *And this gospel of the kingdom will be preached in the whole world as a testimony to all nations, and then the end will come.* What Christ describes about his return in that chapter will happen only when the Gospel has been preached throughout the world.

What we can expect when we are serious about the Great Commission

- Preaching focused on the kingdom of God.
- Making disciples as the primary work of the church.
- Baptism in water as an integral part of ministry, as the sign of forgiveness of sins, the death of the old nature, and our union with Christ.
- Study and teaching of everything Jesus said, with the goal of obedience.

For years, evangelistic crusades (most famously with Billy Graham) solicited the involvement of every church in the area. Churches would set aside their differences and work together for a while, with all their energy focused on the crusade. If we are going to complete the Great Commission, we need every believer involved, capable leaders, churches providing solid discipleship, and all the spiritual gifts operating. That means the Body of Christ must be healthy and in top shape, like an athlete getting ready to run the most important race of his life. We are preparing the bride for the wedding of the Lamb!

Fulfilling the Great Commission does not mean big crusades, distributing the New Testament to everyone, podcasts and TV programs, or visits to every household on the planet. Those things may be good, but they are not what Christ describes as our commission.

So what should you be doing?

There are many options! So many that it becomes confusing! And there is truth in each one. Like the body Paul describes in 1 Corinthians 12, some are feet, some hands, etc. On their own, they are dysfunctional. To function properly, we need every member of the body working in a coordinated and united effort to complete the Great Commission. Jesus does not make it complicated, but many believers' lives would be transformed if they focused on just two things:

1. Walking every day like Jesus walked.
2. Working to fulfill the Great Commission.

Leaders are needed if we are to fulfill the Great Commission

It is time to raise up leaders in the church who follow Jesus' teachings and example instead of secular models of leadership. You may say: "But I'm not a leader!" It is true that not everyone is a leader; in fact, there are many more followers than there are leaders. There is a variety of gifts and callings: not everyone is an apostle or pastor—some have less visible gifts, such as service or administration. God has given more talents or abilities to some people than to others, but God wants every believer to be a servant: *"Whoever wants to become great among you must be your servant, and whoever wants to be first must be your slave— just as the Son of Man did not come to be served, but to serve, and to give his life as a ransom for many"* (Matt. 20:26–28).

In itself, being busy with the work Jesus entrusted to his disciples (the Twelve and the Seventy-two) does not guarantee God's blessing. What is essential is to do God's will: *"Not everyone who says to me, 'Lord, Lord,' will enter the kingdom of heaven, but only the one who does the will of my Father who is in heaven. Many will say to me on that day, 'Lord, Lord, did we not prophesy in your name and in your name drive out demons and in your name perform many miracles?'"* (Matt. 7:21–22). God has something for you to do. The consequences of not doing his will are ugly and eternal. Read this book prayerfully: "Lord, what is your will for me? What part do I have in fulfilling the Great Commission?"

The importance of fruit in the Christian life

John the Baptist warned the Jews of the danger of unfruitfulness: *The ax is already at the root of the trees, and every tree that does not produce good fruit will be cut down and thrown into the fire* (Matt. 3:10). Jesus said the same thing to all his disciples in the Sermon on the Mount: *"Every tree that does not bear good fruit is cut down and thrown into the fire"* (Matt. 7:19). In the parable of the seed and four types of soil, the only good soil is the fruitful soil. There are various levels of harvest, but fruit is required: *"But the seed falling on good soil refers to someone who hears the word and understands it. This is the one who produces a crop, yielding a hundred, sixty or thirty times what was sown"* (Matt. 13:23). You, along with every Christian, are salt and light wherever God has placed you. He wants to use your life to benefit his kingdom. It could be talking with someone at work, taking care of a sick neighbor, or teaching the Word to your son.

The natural result of abiding or remaining in Christ and being close to him is to be very fruitful; the one who does not abide cannot bear fruit and will be cut off and burned (in hell): *"I am the vine; you are the branches. If you remain in me and I in you, you will bear much fruit; apart from me you can do nothing. If you do not remain in me, you are like a branch that is thrown away and withers; such branches are picked up, thrown into the fire and burned"* (Jn. 15:5–6). The person with a broader calling will receive a more extensive ministry: *"Whoever has will be given more, and they will have an abundance. Whoever does not have, even what they have will be taken from them"* (Matt. 13:12).

The importance of our works in the epistles

God has entrusted the message of salvation to all believers. To those who claim that not everyone is called to evangelize, Peter says: *Always be prepared to give an answer to everyone who asks you to give the reason for the hope that you have. But do this with gentleness and respect* (1 Pet. 3:15). You are Christ's ambassador. Taking this message to the world is a significant part of being a Christian:

All this is from God, who reconciled us to himself through Christ and gave us the ministry of reconciliation: that God was reconciling the world to himself in Christ, not counting people's sins against them. And he has committed to us the message of reconciliation. We are therefore Christ's ambassadors, as though God were making his appeal through us. We implore you on Christ's behalf: Be reconciled to God (2 Cor. 5:18–20).

Leaders are not the only priests; we are all part of a chosen race and a royal priesthood, tasked with proclaiming God's works: *But you are a chosen people, a royal priesthood, a holy nation, God's special possession, that you may declare the praises of him who called you out of darkness into his wonderful light* (1 Pet. 2:9). Church leaders do not do all the ministry and evangelism; their job is to equip the whole church to do the work of ministry. That includes evangelism and supernatural ministry in the world, but the emphasis in Ephesians 4 is on building up the body of Christ: *So Christ himself gave the apostles, the prophets, the evangelists, the pastors and teachers,* **to equip his people for works of service,** *so that the body of Christ may be built up* (Eph. 4:11–12).

The natural result of our faith is good deeds: *In the same way, faith by itself, if it is not accompanied by works, is dead* (Jm. 2:17). While the church has priority in your service, every Christian is called to do good to all people: *Let us not become weary in doing good, for at the proper time we will reap a harvest if we do not give up. Therefore, as we have opportunity, let us do good to all people, especially to those who belong to the family of believers* (Galatians 6:9-10). God created you to do good works, which he has already prepared for you: *For we are God's handiwork, created in Christ Jesus to do good works, which God prepared in advance for us to do* (Eph. 2:10). Enjoying God's blessings is part of being a Christian, but in the measure as the blessing we have received, we are to be rich in good deeds:

Command those who are rich in this present world not to be arrogant nor to put their hope in wealth, which is so uncertain, but to put their hope in God, who richly provides us with everything for our enjoyment. Command them to do good, to be rich in good deeds, and to be generous and willing to share. In this way they will lay up treasure for themselves as a firm foundation for the coming age, so that they may take hold of the life that is truly life (1 Tim. 6:17–19).

Are you convinced God has something for you to do in his kingdom? That you have a role in completing the Great Commission? This parable should eliminate any lingering doubt.

The parable of the talents

This passage in Matthew 25 (and another similar parable in Luke 19:12–27) is possibly the most explicit teaching about every believer's responsibility to be fruitful (a deeper study of all of Matthew 25 is found in chapter 23 of the previous volume in this series).

As the master leaves on a journey, he entrusts his servants with his money, in varying quantities:

14 "Again, it will be like a man going on a journey, who called his servants and entrusted his wealth to them. 15 To one he gave five bags of gold, to another two bags, and to another one bag, each according to his ability. Then he went on his journey.

Traditionally, we have followed the King James Version and called this the parable of the talents, which makes us think of abilities. It can include that, along with spiritual gifts, time, or any other resource, but Jesus was talking about money. They received different amounts, according to their abilities. Nobody received more or less than what God knew they could use. The parable in Luke contains the same message, but there are ten men, and everyone receives the same amount of money.

16 The man who had received five bags of gold went at once and put his money to work and gained five bags more. 17 So also, the one with two bags of gold gained two more. 18 But the man who had received one bag went off, dug a hole in the ground and hid his master's money.

Nobody lost or wasted the master's money. The one who received the most took the most initiative: He went to work *at once* with his money. Only the servant who received one bag did nothing; he hid it.

What have you done with your talent?

The day will come—when Christ returns, at death, or possibly earlier—when we have to give account to God for how we have used what he has given us:

[19] *"After a long time the master of those servants returned and settled accounts with them.* [20] *The man who had received five bags of gold brought the other five. 'Master,' he said, 'you entrusted me with five bags of gold. See, I have gained five more.'*

[21] *"His master replied, 'Well done, good and faithful servant! You have been faithful with a few things; I will put you in charge of many things. Come and share your master's happiness!'*

[22] *"The man with two bags of gold also came. 'Master,' he said, 'you entrusted me with two bags of gold; see, I have gained two more.'*

[23] *"His master replied, 'Well done, good and faithful servant! You have been faithful with a few things; I will put you in charge of many things. Come and share your master's happiness!'*

The quantity of fruit was proportional to the gift; God is happy with the person who does what he can with what he has been given. It is not how much we have, but what we do with what we have. Don't envy the person who has ten talents and get discouraged or angry because you only have one. God will put the person who has been faithful *"in charge"* of much more. God has made us in his image; he expects us to be fruitful, and will reward us with multiplied responsibilities.

In Luke, where each servant received the same amount, one multiplied it ten times, another only five times. But that does not matter; they are rewarded according to what they were able to do with their abilities. They were given the governance of cities (ten for the one who earned ten times, and five for the one who earned five times). We were made to govern, and it is what God expects of a faithful servant (to learn more about that, read my book on King Saul's life, Made to Reign).

The situation is very different for the servant who did nothing with what God gave him; God does not accept excuses for not using your gift:

[24] *"Then the man who had received one bag of gold came. 'Master,' he said, 'I knew that you are a hard man, harvesting where you have not sown and gathering where you have not scattered seed.* [25] *So I was afraid and went out and hid your gold in the ground. See, here is what belongs to you.'*

[26] *"His master replied, 'You wicked, lazy servant! So you knew that I harvest where I have not sown and gather where I have not scattered seed?* [27] *Well then, you should have put my money on deposit with the bankers, so that when I returned I would have received it back with interest.*

This servant had a negative attitude toward his master, and was afraid. The wicked servant in Luke did the same thing. Their laziness and dislike of the master was the issue; saying that it was too much and they were overwhelmed by it is no excuse. The result of not using your gift is losing it; it is given to someone who knows how to use it, and you are condemned to hell:

28 "'So take the bag of gold from him and give it to the one who has ten bags. 29 For whoever has will be given more, and they will have an abundance. Whoever does not have, even what they have will be taken from them. 30 And throw that worthless servant outside, into the darkness, where there will be weeping and gnashing of teeth.'

The fruitful person is given more—God wants him to have an abundance, but he has to work for it. God calls the servant who did nothing "worthless." Although some people may not be able to do much (they lack many talents or abilities), God expects some fruit from every one of his servants. We are servants, called to serve God. It is not optional. You are a steward of what God has given you; when you waste it, don't take care of it, or don't use it, you are in sin and rebellion, and you can expect a harsh punishment.

- What talents have you received? What other resources do you have that can be used for God's kingdom?
- What are you doing with those abilities?
- What is your record of past fruitfulness?
- Are you convinced God wants fruit in your life?
- Are you useful to God? Or worthless?

You have a part in completing the Great Commission

It is vitally important to walk with Jesus and experience life in his kingdom to begin the work of completing the Great Commission. There are too many examples of people zealous to evangelize and do mission work who do not walk like Jesus walked. That character and maturity are essential. Every Christian should reflect their Lord's character and do the things he did. It is beautiful to have a living relationship with Jesus and enjoy life in his kingdom, and it is essential. But there is more: Jesus is calling you to work and be fruitful. The unfruitful tree is cast into the fire.

The Bible makes it clear that every Christian has a part in completing the Great Commission. Not everyone is a leader, but Christ has prepared good works for you and has equipped you with gifts and the power of the Holy Spirit for that ministry. Not everyone will go to the ends of the earth, but everyone is Christ's ambassador, whether in Jerusalem, Samaria, or to other countries. Every Christian should want others to experience the same salvation and new life that they are experiencing. Every believer has an opportunity to lead, whether it is on the job, in the community, at church, or as a mother at home with her children. Moses did not think he was a leader (only of some sheep!), but he encountered God in a burning bush and his life was changed. This book may be your burning bush.

1

The First Steps in Jesus' Ministry

John 1:26–51

While the devil was tempting Jesus in the wilderness, John was baptizing repentant sinners in preparation for the Messiah's arrival. Now it was time for John to introduce this unknown (but vastly superior) person. There is much for us to learn about walking as Jesus walked in these first days of his ministry.

26 "I baptize with water," John replied, "but among you stands one you do not know. 27 He is the one who comes after me, the straps of whose sandals I am not worthy to untie."

Preparing the way for Jesus: Repentance and humility

Are you ready for a living relationship with Jesus? Unfortunately, many "believers" today have never experienced a genuine repentance. Why do I say that?

- They have never humbled themselves, acknowledging the depth of their sin and confessing their need for God.

- They are not broken-hearted for what they have done to God and other people.

- Instead of hating sin and forsaking it, they tolerate sin that separates them from God.

- They go back and forth between the broad road of the world and the straight and narrow way (Matt. 7:13–14), but many of them spend more time on the broad way.

God wants to lift you up, but first you must humble yourself. We see John's humility, something that many ministers lack. Instead of realizing they are unworthy, they think they are special—even indispensable—in God's kingdom. They build great temples and preach prosperity, but do not know what it is to wash the feet of the lowly. God may have given you a beautiful, fruitful, and blessed ministry, but be careful of exaggerating your importance or the importance of your ministry. We are only servants of the Master. Like John, we are preparing his way, to return to this earth and reign with glory and power as the King of kings. We are unworthy of the great privilege of representing him in this world as his ambassadors, but by his grace, he calls and equips us to serve him.

Are you aware that we are to prepare the way for Christ's return? Do you preach repentance and humility to prepare people to receive Jesus? How is your humility? Do you believe that you have experienced a genuine repentance?

To walk as Jesus walked is to walk incognito

Jesus was standing among them, but they did not know it! Jesus' name is not even mentioned in the first sixteen verses of this

Gospel! John said Jesus was so great that he was unworthy even to untie his sandals, yet his identity was a mystery! It is natural to seek the world's acclaim as a successful pastor, but Jesus did nothing to grab the attention of those around him or detract from John's ministry.

Twice (in vv. 31 and 33), John says, "*I myself did not know him.*" That is strange, since John leaped in his mother's womb when he heard Mary's voice. They were cousins, and we can assume they would have spent time together growing up, but somehow John never really knew him. It is possible to be close to Jesus and not know him; it is even more common to have some knowledge of him but not walk as he walked.

Jesus is also standing among us. How sad to have someone so special among us and not know who he is! Even worse is to sing his praises without really knowing him! Just as the religious leaders in John's day did not know Jesus, it is possible to have a great ministry, but never know him (Matt. 7:21–23).

You may have a word or a calling from God, but you are still unknown and walking incognito. That is okay. Nobody knew Jesus either—even his own family did not really know him!

Jesus revealed

28 This all happened at Bethany on the other side of the Jordan, where John was baptizing.

The people with John did not have to wait long for this mysterious person to be revealed:

29 The next day John saw Jesus coming toward him and said, "Look, the Lamb of God, who takes away the sin of the world! 30 This is the one I meant when I said, 'A man who comes after me has surpassed me because he was before me.' 31 I myself did not know him, but the reason I came baptizing with water was that he might be revealed to Israel."

To walk as Jesus walked is to be submissive

John himself said that Jesus was superior to him, but Jesus voluntarily submitted to John, giving him preference so John could complete his ministry, and submitting to John's baptism:

Then Jesus came from Galilee to the Jordan to be baptized by John. But John tried to deter him, saying, "I need to be baptized by you, and do you come to me?" Jesus replied, "Let it be so now; it is proper for us to do this to fulfill all righteousness." Then John consented. As soon as Jesus was baptized, he went up out of the water. At that moment heaven was opened, and he saw the Spirit of God descending like a dove and alighting on him. And a voice from heaven said, "This is my Son, whom I love; with him I am well pleased" (Matt. 3:13–17).

When we walk as Jesus walked, we submit to God-established authority; particularly to God, but also to pastors or apostles God has placed in our lives. Humility is expressed in taking the lower place and not seeking a special position.

John said that the reason he baptized with water was to reveal Jesus to Israel. Jesus did not need to repent, but something happened spiritually in his baptism that released that revelation: The Holy Spirit descended on him, and he received the Father's approval.

To walk like Jesus is costly

Jesus' submission to the Father's purpose was very costly. It sounds nice to be the sweet "Lamb of God," and very noble to "take away the sins of the world," but being a lamb meant being a sacrifice. Jesus paid the price of our sin with his own blood. He died on the cross as a propitiation for our sin, to redeem us and reconcile us with God.

Have you paid a high price to serve Jesus? Have you had to deny yourself or sacrifice something to follow him?

To walk as Jesus walked is to emphasize the forgiveness of sin

John gives two purposes for Jesus' coming. The first is to take away the sin of the whole world, because *God so loved the world that he gave his one and only Son, that whoever believes in him shall not perish but have eternal life* (Jn. 3:16). When you share Jesus with someone, do you help them understand the nature and seriousness of sin? Do you include forgiveness of sin as the foundation for a God-pleasing life? Are you committed to bringing that message to the whole world? Has Jesus taken your sins away?

32 Then John gave this testimony: "I saw the Spirit come down from heaven as a dove and remain on him. 33 And I myself did not know him, but the one who sent me to baptize with water told me, 'The man on whom you see the Spirit come down and remain is the one who will baptize with the Holy Spirit.' 34 I have seen and I testify that this is God's Chosen One."

To walk as Jesus walked is to wait for God's timing

Jesus spent almost twenty years in preparation, patiently (we assume) awaiting the moment that his Father would release him to start his ministry. He had to allow another minister (John) to prepare the way for him. If your ministry seems to be on hold, it may be that God has someone else preparing the way for it.

There are also times when we have to recognize and accept that the ministry God gave us has been completed—it is time for us to step back and support someone else, perhaps much greater, whom God has revealed to us. We must be obedient at that point and yield to them. John was not in competition with Jesus. It would have been foolish for him to insist on continuing his ministry of baptism in water while Jesus was baptizing in the Spirit. Unfortunately, many people do not want to let go of a ministry whose time is over. To walk as Jesus walked is to trust and rest in the Father's sovereignty. He is in charge. He knows all things and has everything in his hands.

To walk as Jesus walked is to emphasize the Holy Spirit

John baptized multitudes, but he knew that something much greater was on the way: the Holy Spirit. The second purpose John gives for Jesus' ministry is to baptize with the Holy Spirit. Jesus commanded us to baptize with water as a symbol of our identification with his death and resurrection (Matt. 28:19). That baptism is different than John's baptism of repentance, and is an important symbol of the new birth. However, there is another baptism which is even more important, the baptism of the Spirit, to fill you with the third person of the Trinity and immerse you in God's love and power. If we are to walk as Jesus walked, we have to preach and administer that baptism. How sad that we often ignore it! Even in Pentecostal or charismatic churches, the baptism is seldom mentioned, and many believers have never experienced it. The Spirit had to *come down* and *remain* on Jesus. It is great when the Spirit comes down to touch you in an anointed service! But it is even better when he remains on (or in) you. It is impossible to walk as Jesus walked without the baptism of the Holy Spirit. For an in-depth study of the Spirit, read my book <u>What Ever Happened to the Baptism in the Holy Spirit</u>?

To walk as Jesus walked is to make disciples

35 The next day John was there again with two of his disciples. 36 When he saw Jesus passing by, he said, "Look, the Lamb of God!"

37 When the two disciples heard him say this, they followed Jesus.

John had disciples, and now Jesus gets his first disciples. Later, he commanded us to make disciples:

"Therefore go and make disciples of all nations, baptizing them in the name of the Father and of the Son and of the Holy Spirit, and teaching them to obey everything I have commanded you. And surely I am with you always, to the very end of the age (Matt. 28:19–20)."

This was a test of John's humility: he proclaimed Jesus as the Lamb of God, and then lost two of his disciples to him! Losing sheep to another ministry is always painful; "sheep stealers" are looked down upon. But Jesus did not steal them; John let them go. It is hard, but there may be times when we have to release someone in the church to move to another ministry where they can do more for the kingdom.

38 Turning around, Jesus saw them following and asked, "What do you want?"

They said, "Rabbi" (which means "Teacher"), "where are you staying?"

It is tempting to immediately receive someone who comes from another church to be part of your ministerial team, but it is wise to ask them: "What do you want?" Jesus wanted to know where their hearts were at.

They were not seeking position or power; they only wanted to know where Jesus was staying, go to his house, and be with him. That pleased Jesus. We do not seek him for his blessings, a miracle, success in ministry, or prosperity. We just want to be with him and dwell in his presence.

39 "Come," he replied, "and see."

So they went and saw where he was staying, and they spent that day with him. It was about four in the afternoon.

These are Jesus' first disciples! Finally! How exciting! But Jesus takes it easy, and just invites them to *"come and see."* No commitment. No promise of being part of a great ministry. First, they have to obey the command to go to where Jesus is, and then observe him. In the same way, we invite interested people to God's house, allow them to see Jesus, and observe how he impacts and transforms people. In this case, they stayed with him, as we expect would happen when someone sees Jesus in all his glory. Who would want to leave Jesus' side? When someone comes to your church, can they see Jesus? Or only a professional worship band, a great preacher, or a beautiful building? If they do not stay, could it be that it is hard to see Jesus amid all the smoke and noise?

If you have the opportunity to invite someone to your home, hopefully, they will see a Christ-centered marriage, children who honor their parents, and the peace of Christ. That hospitality is important, but be sure your family is safe, and the visitors do not disrupt your family time.

The first evangelists

40 Andrew, Simon Peter's brother, was one of the two who heard what John had said and who had followed Jesus. 41 The first thing Andrew did was to find his brother Simon and tell him, "We have found the Messiah" (that is, the Christ). **⁴²** *And he brought him to Jesus.*

Jesus looked at him and said, "You are Simon son of John. You will be called Cephas" (which, when translated, is Peter).

When you find something as life-changing as Jesus, you have to share the news with your family. Andrew was the first evangelist. Jesus did not call Peter or seek out the man who would be the leader of the disciples. His brother sought him out, shared the good news with him, and brought him to Jesus.

Jesus did not see a fisherman; he saw a rock and Peter's potential. When we walk as Jesus walked, we see everyone who comes our way with new eyes. Each one is important. As we truly look at them, the Lord may give us a word of knowledge about them, a life-changing word. You may have the opportunity to release a destiny and a calling in a young person's life.

When you walk like Jesus, you can say: Follow me

⁴³ *The next day Jesus decided to leave for Galilee. Finding Philip, he said to him, "Follow me."*

Jesus was starting something that would include millions of people, but he began with one person at a time. We saw those first disciples' interest in Jesus and where he was staying; now Jesus took the initiative, and commanded Philip: *"Follow me."* To be Jesus' disciple is to follow him. When we decide to obey, we start a pilgrimage on that narrow road to heaven. We must keep our eyes on Jesus and follow him wherever he goes.

It may feel awkward to ask someone to follow you. Of course, they must follow Jesus, but we also need flesh-and-blood models. When you walk as Jesus walked, you can call someone to follow you, trusting that the other person will see Jesus in you and will seek him. God may also show you someone you can invite or call to be part of a ministry team.

Are you walking in such a way that you feel confident asking someone to follow you?

[44] *Philip, like Andrew and Peter, was from the town of Bethsaida.* [45] *Philip found Nathanael and told him, "We have found the one Moses wrote about in the Law, and about whom the prophets also wrote—Jesus of Nazareth, the son of Joseph."*

When you witness to someone, you do not need great knowledge of the Word or a profound message, although biblical knowledge is valuable, and you should do everything you can to prepare yourself. You can simply share what you have experienced. Unfortunately, you will not always get a positive response:

[46] *"Nazareth! Can anything good come from there?" Nathanael asked.*

Not everyone will share your enthusiasm about Jesus. You will encounter prejudice, at times, because the person belongs to another church or religion, or because of hypocrites they have known. There is no need to condemn, get into arguments, or preach at them. Philip responded very wisely:

"Come and see," said Philip.

Walking like Jesus, you will invite others to come to him and see him

Philip was already walking like Jesus! He said exactly what Jesus had said the day before! When a person takes that step of faith to seek God, the Holy Spirit is released to reveal Christ. If they have open eyes (and hearts), they will see amazing things.

47 When Jesus saw Nathanael approaching, he said of him, "Here truly is an Israelite in whom there is no deceit."

Jesus knew that Nathanael would be a tough case. His skepticism was probably apparent, but Jesus knew how to engage him in conversation. It might look like flattery, but saying something positive (and true) to a person is a great way to get their attention.

Jesus was an expert in studying people. Apart from his supernatural ability to see what was inside someone, I am sure he read Nathanael's body language, something many people ignore. Pay close attention to eyes, facial expressions, and posture, and respond accordingly.

To walk like Jesus is to operate in supernatural revelation

God can give anyone a gift of prophecy or word of knowledge, to say something that only God could reveal. Think the best about others, and look beyond appearances, to the heart.

48 "How do you know me?" Nathanael asked.

Jesus had not won Nathanael over yet; he was still defensive, but now a supernatural revelation would break through his tough exterior:

Jesus answered, "I saw you while you were still under the fig tree before Philip called you."

49 Then Nathanael declared, "Rabbi, you are the Son of God; you are the king of Israel."

What a drastic change! Sometimes the people who are most skeptical end up being the most committed to Jesus. Nathanael was not closed—he just needed to make sure this man was authentic.

⁵⁰ Jesus said, "You believe because I told you I saw you under the fig tree. You will see greater things than that." ⁵¹ He then added, "Very truly I tell you, you will see 'heaven open, and the angels of God ascending and descending on' the Son of Man."

Walking with Jesus, you will see heaven opened and the glory of God

Are you ready to see greater things? Are you ready for an open heaven? Do you believe that if you are walking with Jesus, you will see amazing things?

What grabs your attention about Jesus here? How can you follow his example? Do you believe that God can give you a word of knowledge about someone that will bring them to Jesus' feet? Do you want to walk like Jesus walked?

2

The Master's Plan

Christ did many things while he walked this earth:

- Taught about life in the kingdom.
- Explained the law and summarized it in two commands: love God and love your neighbor.
- Healed the sick.
- Delivered the demonized.

The great news is that as we walk with Jesus, we can teach his word and help people obey it. We can heal the sick and set the demonized free. However, Jesus probably devoted only a few hours a day to teaching and miracles.

The most important thing Jesus did was unique: bearing the world's sin as he died on the cross and purchased our salvation with his blood. Nothing else Jesus did can compare with the importance of that atoning sacrifice, but he accomplished it in the matter of a few days. There is no way we can repeat it, although we can tell the world the good news.

So if you are going to walk like Jesus walked, what should you spend your time doing? Aside from his saving death, the most important thing Jesus did was pour his life into the twelve disciples.

To my sisters in Christ reading this, in no way do I intend to exclude you. As a spiritual father (and former prison chaplain), I am used to working with men, and this chapter is oriented toward men. Most of these principles can apply to women as well, possibly with some slight changes. It is wise to maintain same-sex discipling relationships. The need for spiritual mothers discipling younger women in the Lord is just as great as the need for spiritual fathers. The command to make disciples is certainly not limited to men!

God's multiplication strategy

Fortunately, you and I can also pour our lives into others, and it should probably have the same priority in the use of our time. Jesus' strategy has been written about in books like Robert Coleman's The Master Plan of Evangelism (http://cciog.com/wp-content/uploads/2014/12/TheMasterPlanOfEvangelism.pdf), and Dawson Trotman's Born to Reproduce (http://www.discipleshiplibrary.com/pdfs/AA094.pdf).

The church has spent billions of dollars on seminars, books, and training materials. Billions more on TV networks, crusades, and movies. Obviously, they have impacted many lives, but as I have been drawn back to Christ's simplicity, I cannot help but think that we have lost sight of the fundamental (and free) strategy that Jesus used so effectively. It is the simple relationship of a more mature believer with a younger Christian. Notice I say "more mature," because a six-month-old Christian who is being mentored can help someone come to Christ and start encouraging them in their walk with the Lord. It does not take extensive training. Age is irrelevant, and you do not need to be a spiritual giant and have it all together.

How to fulfill the Great Commission in your lifetime

I want to impress on you a startling statistic that has captured my imagination for years. The amazing possibilities for impacting a nation are so obvious, I cannot figure out why we do not pay more attention to it. Perhaps the enemy has deceived us because he knows how powerful it is. All I have to do is disciple one man this year. Next year, he disciples just one man, while I start with someone new. Each year, everyone finds just one new man to disciple. You do not forget about the man you discipled the previous year—maintain that relationship while you focus on the next disciple. After ten years, I will have discipled ten men, but if each is faithful to follow the model, these will be the numbers reached:

After 10 years: 1000

After 20 years: One MILLION

After 30 years: One BILLION

That all starts with me, with one person. We are not talking about "decisions," we are talking about solid disciples of Jesus Christ. Even if only half of the people discipled are faithful to help someone else, I will have reached 500 million in 30 years!

Why not do what Jesus commanded us to do?

Go and make disciples of all nations, baptizing them in the name of the Father and of the Son and of the Holy Spirit, and teaching them to obey everything I have commanded you. (Matt. 28:19–20)

Jesus never told us to build big organizations or beautiful temples. He told us to make disciples. We need to follow Jesus' plan. The last thing we need is another new, improved way of doing church.

Earlier accounts in the Gospels (Matt. 4:18–22; Mk. 1:16–20; Lk. 5:1–11) recount the calling of the first disciples, but the actual designation of the Twelve comes later. The number twelve was highly significant to the Jews because of their twelve patriarchs and tribes. Jesus could handle twelve. I am suggesting you start with one. Of course, if God leads, you can work with more, but it seems like any more than twelve would be very difficult.

Now, following this simple model, how could we make disciples of every person on this planet by 2030, when the population is estimated to reach 8.5 billion? We could make disciples of every one in ten years and fulfill the Great Commission if we start now (when this was written in 2019), with 8.5 million believers following this model. Realistically, we might need ten years to train them, so we believe God for 8,500 people prepared to make disciples this year. Even if we need another ten years to get the necessary materials, Bibles, and funding, we could fulfill the Commission in thirty years.

Of course, we do not know God's timing, and we do not want to impose our program on God or anyone else. We do not need another agenda, program, or "apostle" to organize this and spend millions promoting his plan around the world. God does not work that way. I am very confident that God can manage it. His Holy Spirit can move all the people and resources that are necessary; we just need to be faithful and walk as Jesus walked. We know that not everyone will accept Christ; in fact, they will be a minority. However, it does give us a vision of the power of the Master's plan.

3

Let's Do It!

Where do we start? When do we start? Why put it off any more? Are you unsure of what Jesus meant? Still unconvinced? As clear as Jesus' strategy is—and as effective as he proved it be—for some reason, it seems we do everything possible to avoid taking the simple steps to implement it. I will warn you: It takes faith, the anointing of the Holy Spirit, and a lot of hard work. If you have already begun walking like Jesus walked after reading the first two books, this is the logical next step.

So what is the problem?

If this is the key to reaching the world for Christ, and if the Father is just waiting for the completion of the Great Commission to send Jesus back to this earth, it makes total sense that Satan will do everything in his power to stop it.

Expect all kinds of questions and condemnation from others when you start. Through the centuries there has been much abuse and perversion of discipling. The world is only too familiar with the sexual abuse scandals regarding the formation of priests in the Catholic church. The intimacy of the relationship can give ungodly men opportunities to control, manipulate, and abuse sincere young men. In the 1970's the "Shepherding Movement" got a bad name because of the control "elders" exercised over those they were shepherding. Recently there have been multiple reports of problems with the emerging movement of "apostles," those providing "spiritual covering," and "spiritual fathers." Some demand payment, absolute loyalty, or unhealthy submission to their every desire. Don't let the excesses—which unfortunately exist every time there is a move of God—keep you from doing what God has called you to do.

The New Testament is clear on the role of apostles in supervising churches and their leaders. Paul repeatedly exerted his authority over the churches he founded. The church has always had some form of discipleship. When I was on staff with Inter-Varsity Christian Fellowship, we called them Paul/Timothy relationships. The concept of spiritual father has not been common in the North American church. I had never been called that until I worked as a prison chaplain in Puerto Rico, where men who came to Christ and were growing in grace under my ministry would call me their spiritual father. It is a widespread practice in Latin America, although it too has been twisted and abused. Paul said of the Corinthians, *Even if you had ten thousand guardians in Christ, you do not have many fathers, for in Christ Jesus I became your father through the gospel* (1 Cor. 4:15). Paul addresses his disciple, *To Timothy, my dear son* (1 Tim. 1:2), and again, *You then, my son, be strong in the grace that is in Christ Jesus* (2 Tim. 2:1). The nature of their relationship is evident in these references: *Timothy, my son, I am giving you this command in keeping with the prophecies once made about you* (1 Tim. 1:18) and *For this reason I have sent to you Timothy, my son whom I love, who is faithful in the Lord. He will remind you of my way of life in Christ Jesus, which agrees with what I teach everywhere in every church* (1 Cor. 4:17).

Allow the Holy Spirit to confirm what he wants for you. When you are ready, here are some practical steps to begin, based on what

Jesus did. As important as making disciples is in Jesus' strategy, in my fifty years as a Christian, I have heard very few teachings on how to actually do it.

The first step in choosing a disciple

Luke 6:12 gives us important background, which Mark and Matthew omit:

One of those days Jesus went out to a mountainside to pray, and spent the night praying to God.

Jesus already had disciples following him, but officially designating some as apostles is so important that he spent an entire night talking with his Father, the only recorded time that he prayed all night. Though the selection of your "disciple" may seem obvious, get away to a quiet place where you can think and pray without interruptions. Turn off the phone (maybe even take a retreat), and spend serious time in communion with God. This is a decision that will change someone's life (and yours!).

Mark 3 gives the simple framework for initiating a discipling relationship:

[13] Jesus went up on a mountainside and called to him those he wanted, and they came to him.

Jesus called those he wanted to him

- The initiative lies with you, the spiritual father or mother. Do not wait for someone to come and ask to be discipled.

- Do not feel bad about being selective. You do not have to make a big deal out of who you choose. Many people will not understand what you are doing and will question your motives in selecting one and not another. Do not let that discourage you.

- The one who was not chosen may be jealous. Do not do anything that would encourage that jealousy, but stand firm on what you believe God has called you to do.

- What if the person refuses? They may feel uncomfortable being singled out. If they refuse, it is probably time to go back to the Lord in prayer. Maybe they just need some time to pray and think it over.

- Be careful of how you present it. Do not put demands on them—no need to say: "I believe God has called me to be your spiritual father." Usually, that relationship will be natural. Most of my "spiritual sons" already saw me as their spiritual father before I initiated a more intensive discipleship, usually because I had led them to the Lord.

- Though Jesus' example puts the burden on the mentor to initiate the relationship, some people may be shy about doing that. There is nothing wrong with you approaching someone and asking them to disciple you. Then it is on them to pray about it for God's confirmation. Do not be devastated if they say they already have all they can handle and turn you down! Keep praying that God would provide someone.

They came to him

- Be careful of making the relationship too intense. Even though Jesus may be guiding you to call someone, you are not Jesus. They have the freedom to come to you, or not. Let God deal with them if they choose not to come. If they choose to end the relationship, do not put a guilt trip on them.

- There should be an eagerness on the part of the younger believer. Be careful of trying to create something that is not there. Acceptance of your invitation often confirms that you have heard the Lord.

- Beware of any inclination to control him or use him for your own benefit. Christ laid down his life for his disciples, and we should be ready to do the same. If you are the disciple, beware of any attempt by a spiritual father to control you. It can be very difficult to see troubling changes in someone you have grown to love and who has had an impact on your life, but do not let that blind you to the possibility of spiritual abuse. Unfortunately, it is rampant in the church today.

- Jesus never asked for a penny from any of his disciples, nor should you. You should never be expected to give money for an apostolic covering, discipling, or mentoring.

14 He appointed twelve – designating them apostles – that they might be with him and that he might send them out to preach 15 and to have authority to drive out demons.

He appointed twelve and designated them apostles

- The Twelve were a clearly defined group, with an inner circle of three (Peter, James, and John). Part of growth in Christ is accepting your call and resisting envy of those with a higher calling. The disciples fell into the fleshly "who is the greatest?" game like many believers do today.

- Though Jesus was not big on titles, there may be a place in some churches for designating people for specific functions. Depending on their role, it may be important for the church to know that the person has your support.

That they might be with Jesus

- The most important part of mentoring is simply being together. Jesus spent extensive time with his disciples, some of whom were married. It is essential to do more than a weekly meeting. Get to know their family. Visit their job. Go to the gym or do something fun together. Have him in your home so he can observe you relating to your family.

- Yes, that can put pressure on you to "walk as Jesus walked." It is not that hard to sound spiritual in an hour-long meeting as you study Scripture and pray together. They need to see you at your best and your worst. That is OK. You do not have to be perfect. Be real, but by God's grace, try to be a good example.

He sent them out to preach

- Spend time with him talking and praying about his calling and gifting. You want to encourage him to develop and use those gifts. Never hold him back out of jealousy! If he goes on to a greater ministry elsewhere, praise God!

- Give him opportunities to stretch his spiritual muscles, whether it is preaching in church, going together on a mission trip, evangelizing, or some other practical experience. Make sure you adequately prepare him and debrief afterward.

He gave them authority to heal and drive out demons

- One of the most important things we can foster in a young man is spiritual authority, and appropriate authority in his family. Jesus started the Great

Commission in Matthew 28 by saying, *"All authority in heaven and on earth has been given unto me."* He grants that authority to us as we obey his command to make disciples. We do not grasp authority—we are given it by someone with greater authority. You may be able to grant him that authority in certain situations, or help him grow in his God-given authority.

- Authority can go to a man's head. The disciples talked about calling down fire on unbelievers (Lk. 9:54). Model and teach appropriate authority, and never abuse it.

- Teach the reality of spiritual warfare and how to deal with demons. Make sure he is free of any demonic strongholds! (For more on this, see my book Lessons in Deliverance.)

- Some less reliable manuscripts include the authority to heal. Jesus certainly gave them that authority as well. Healing goes hand in hand with deliverance. You want his life to be filled with God's supernatural power. Encourage him to move into these areas.

God looks at the heart

Mark 3:16–19 lists the disciples, the ones who would walk with Jesus until his death and be responsible for carrying on his mission and establishing the Church. Chapter seven will take a closer look at them, but it is a ragtag bunch that the Father confirmed as Jesus' disciples. Who is missing?

- Anybody religious, such as a priest or Pharisee
- Anyone highly educated (they were *"unlearned and ignorant"*, Acts 4:13)
- Anyone from a prestigious family

- Anyone popular in Israel at that time

Instead, what we see are:

- Several rough and tough fishermen
- A despised tax collector
- Common people
- A couple of disciples of John the Baptist, himself a radical
- A questionable character who would later betray him (was that a wise decision?)

Jesus' choice can be instructive for us as we pray about who to disciple. It reminds me of Samuel anointing the next king from Jesse's family. The prophet was leaning toward the best-looking or oldest, but God said: *"Do not consider his appearance or his height, for I have rejected him. The Lord does not look at the things people look at. People look at the outward appearance, but the Lord looks at the heart"* (1 Sam. 16:7).

God chose David, the youngest, who was out in the fields with the sheep. Often it is not the one who prays the loudest or is the most popular. Seminary or Bible school education may not mean much. It is usually not the one voted most likely to succeed. It may be someone with disabilities, awkward in social situations, or from a minority group. What would I look for?

- Humility: willingness to take the lowest place; not ambitious
- A solid prayer/devotional life
- Consistent lifestyle at home and work
- A heart of love for God, Christian brothers and sisters, and the unsaved
- Availability to be used by God
- Hunger for God's Word
- A teachable spirit

- Honesty about sin and personal struggles
- A heart to worship God in spirit and truth

What's next?

It is a big step to call someone and initiate a discipleship relationship. You need to be committed for the long haul, through the inevitable ups and downs in his life and your relationship. You can damage someone deeply if you start a relationship and then back off when your life gets too busy or it is more than you counted on; too many men had their fathers give up on them.

- You may already be doing this without knowing it; this may just focus what you have been doing.

- Maybe you have been hesitant to initiate a relationship, and this is the gentle push you needed. It is time to get going.

- Maybe you have let a discipling relationship slide, and you need to confess your failure and get things back on track.

- Maybe you were hurt by a spiritual father or mother. God wants to heal that and release you to give another person what you missed out on.

- Maybe there are some uncomfortable things you need to confront in your spiritual son's life. That is part of it. Or those uncomfortable things may be in your own life.

- There may be someone who immediately comes to mind who would welcome this relationship. God may already be preparing both of you.

Making disciples like Jesus did is not common today. A major survey by Lifeway Research in 2019 found that less than half (48%) of US church-goers agree with the statement "I intentionally spend time with other believers to help them grow in their faith." Nearly two-thirds (65%) agreed with the statement, "I can walk with God without other believers." That is tragic, and makes completing the Great Commission much more difficult!

Are you a disciple of Jesus Christ? Have you heard his call? Have you responded to it? He has given you the same opportunity he gave the apostles:

- Jesus wants you to be with him, to share his life with you.
- He is sending you to preach the Good News.
- He is giving you authority to heal and cast out demons.

God can use you to disciple someone! Do not just write off that possibility. Earnestly pray about it. This could be the start of a whole new phase of your walk with Jesus. It is part of walking as Jesus walked.

4

Plentiful Harvest, Few Workers

Matthew 9:35–38

The previous chapters have presented an amazingly simple and effective plan for reaching a billion people in thirty years. Of course, things do not always go according to plan, even for Jesus, and he is God! He knew exactly the right thing to do each step of the way! Judas ended up being a traitor. James was killed shortly after Pentecost—the first apostle martyred. Shockingly, it seems like the Lord of the universe has a recruitment problem. There is far more work to do than there are laborers! No wonder Jesus spent the majority of his time and energy training these twelve men!

In Matthew 10, Jesus sent the apostles out on their first "missionary trip." That chapter is full of important principles we can follow as we disciple someone. However, the chapter division (which was not part of the original text) can cause us to miss the important introduction at the end of chapter 9:

35 Jesus went through all the towns and villages, teaching in their synagogues, proclaiming the good news of the kingdom and healing every disease and sickness.

It is not a coincidence that verse 35 is strikingly similar to Matthew 4:23:

Jesus went throughout Galilee, teaching in their synagogues, proclaiming the good news of the kingdom, and healing every disease and sickness among the people.

Both verses summarize the preceding ministry and introduce the significant teaching section that follows. In the case of Matthew 4, it was the Sermon on the Mount; in chapter 9, it will be the second of the five significant teachings in Matthew.

Every disease

Jesus had been traveling throughout Galilee, teaching, preaching the kingdom, and healing. We know he already had disciples traveling with him, but apparently they were still watching and learning. At this point, Jesus was ministering alone, and there were three important parts to that ministry:

1. **Teaching** the Word of God in the synagogue (today it would be the church) to those who already believe. There is an alarming lack of knowledge, sound interpretation, and practice of the Bible in today's church.

The rest of his ministry was outside the building, with people who were not yet in the kingdom:

2. **Preaching** the good news of the kingdom. We must proclaim that God is the sovereign King and establish his lordship in our lives, our homes, and all of our society. His perfect reign of righteousness and peace will be established when Christ returns.

3. **Healing**. In the Gospels and Acts, there was always a confirmation of the word with signs and wonders. Jesus healed *every* disease and sickness. That is one of those all-encompassing words that cause theologians headaches. *Every* disease. Matthew 4:23 says the same thing, and that word will show up again in the first verse of chapter 10. We are impressed if a couple of people get healed, and readily excuse the failure to heal a difficult disease. Not so with Jesus. No wonder crowds came to him. If we are going to complete the Great Commission, we need to follow Jesus' model.

36 When he saw the crowds, he had compassion on them, because they were harassed and helpless, like sheep without a shepherd.

Harassed and helpless sheep

Jesus was never impressed with crowds. Of course, he was thrilled to see people freed from their suffering, but he knew that the need went much deeper. They need a shepherd. They are lost *sheep that have gone astray, each following his own way* (Is. 53:6). They are harassed and helpless. It is not that hard to post some profound teaching on the internet or get a crowd excited with anointed preaching. When God's power is present, it is not even that hard to minister healing. You may feel drained afterward, but there is the exhilaration of seeing the lame walk and the deaf hear. That is all good. Lots of people love the acclaim that goes with it. However, shepherding sheep is an ongoing, challenging, and often thankless task. You cannot just pray over someone and suddenly they are no longer harassed and helpless. That takes ongoing ministry. It takes compassion. Genuine compassion compels us to move beyond miracles and exciting church services. Compassion moves our hearts to care for hurting people. That is where the workers get hard to find, but that is where the real harvest lies. Without that shepherding, the harvest will be lost. The seed will be snatched by the evil one or smothered by the sheep's daily struggle for survival. The wolf will come in and devour the wandering sheep.

[37] Then he said to his disciples, "The harvest is plentiful but the workers are few.

The harvest is plentiful!

We usually think of the "harvest" as souls in need of salvation, and of course, they are part of the harvest. However, in context, Jesus seems to be talking about his scattered sheep. First, we have a harvest among wayward sheep who already know Jesus. Not many have the patience and compassion to minister to them!

We are quick to point to the godlessness in our society and its resistance to the Gospel, but are we making Jesus out to be a liar? He says the harvest is plentiful! The problem seems to be a shortage of qualified workers. If there is no response, maybe the problem lies in our harvesting methods or the way we have trained the harvesters. We need to do a better job of raising up large numbers of workers so we can see the multiplication that takes place when we follow the Master's plan.

[38] Ask the Lord of the harvest, therefore, to send out workers into his harvest field."

Pray for laborers!

Isn't it interesting that Jesus asks for prayer? Wouldn't you think he could just say the word, and his Father would raise up all the workers he needed? Not so! He partners with us and somehow has chosen to work in response to our prayers. It is easy to pray for God to send workers, as long as I am not one of them! But how can someone with any love in their heart see hurting sheep and hungry people and not go to help them? And perhaps more important, be obedient to the urgent cry of God's heart! We often are motivated to act on what we are praying for. Those who pray fervently for the harvest and the needed workers are more likely to have the compassion to go into the harvest themselves.

The very next verse (10:1) has Jesus calling some of those same disciples he just asked to pray. He gave them authority and sent them out into the harvest. Jesus expects each of us to respond to that prayer! As the disciples moved into the harvest fields, Jesus' ministry would be multiplied.

Lord of the harvest

Remember, God is the Lord of the harvest. It is *his* harvest, not yours, or any particular church's. We are all working for the same Lord of the harvest (hopefully!). More important than filling your own barns is working together to ensure the best harvest, making sure the ripe grain is not lost. Too often, we undermine each other's efforts in an attempt to claim a bigger harvest. God is not pleased if we mess up what he has planted and carefully nurtured!

Are you walking as Jesus walked?

1. Do you follow his example of combining proclamation with demonstration? Are you all talk and little action? Or is there evidence of power over sickness and Satan in your ministry?

2. Do you preach about the kingdom of God? Do you even understand what the kingdom is all about? (See the second book in this series, Kingdom Culture.)

3. Have you seen examples of *every* sickness and disease being healed? If not, why? Can you believe that Jesus would want similar manifestations today?

4. Are you so hung up on miracles and exciting preaching that you ignore the ongoing care for those God has entrusted to you?

5. When is the last time you felt compassion for the people you encounter? Beneath the smiling faces and veneer of victory, can you see the many helpless and harassed sheep? Is there anything you can do about that? Do you even care?

6. What does it mean to shepherd people? How is your church doing at that? How could it be improved?

7. Do you pray regularly for laborers? Are you doing your part? Are you aware of fields ripe for the harvest around you (Jn. 4:35)? Can you help your church see them?

8. Do you approach the harvest with the knowledge that it is God's?

This is exciting, good news! There is a great harvest waiting out there for you! There are plenty of harassed and helpless sheep just waiting for someone to come and care for them! As you continue to disciple someone, you are doing your part to multiply laborers!

5

The First Missionary Journey

Matthew 10:1–20

We heard Jesus' cry for laborers in the final verses of Matthew 9. Even now, his compassionate heart is hurting for the harassed and helpless sheep who have no shepherd. The Father is concerned, because the fields are ripe for harvest—with people whom his Holy Spirit has prepared for salvation—that are going to waste because there are no laborers. Jesus wants to return to earth and establish his kingdom, but he is waiting for laborers who will make disciples throughout the world and fulfill the Great Commission.

Matthew 10 starts very similar to what we covered from Mark 3 in chapter 3:

¹Jesus called his twelve disciples to him and gave them authority to drive out impure spirits and to heal every disease and sickness. ² These are the names of the twelve apostles: first, Simon (who is called Peter) and his brother Andrew; James son of Zebedee, and his brother John; ³ Philip and Bartholomew; Thomas and

Matthew the tax collector; James son of Alphaeus, and Thaddaeus; ⁴ Simon the Zealot and Judas Iscariot, who betrayed him.

In Matthew, Jesus provides detailed instructions for the disciples, which also guide us in evangelism and making disciples. And yes, we do *make* disciples, reflected in the titles of these great books: <u>Disciples</u> <u>are</u> <u>Made</u>, <u>not</u> <u>Born</u> (Walter A. Henrichsen) and <u>The</u> <u>Lost</u> <u>Art</u> <u>of</u> <u>Disciple</u> <u>Making</u> (LeRoy Eims).

Go where God sends you

⁵ These twelve Jesus sent out with the following instructions: "Do not go among the Gentiles or enter any town of the Samaritans. ⁶ Go rather to the lost sheep of Israel.

When God calls, equips, and sends an apostle, missionary, or other minister, they are generally sent to specific people. Do you have any idea who God has sent you to?

As always, we must be careful to interpret the Scripture correctly. Some might infer from Jesus' words that he did not care about Gentiles, and shared the common Jewish disdain for Samaritans. Perhaps some of the apostles' initial hesitancy to believe that the Gospel included the Gentiles came from what Jesus said here, but we know from other Scriptures that Jesus had no such prejudice. In fact, in Acts 1, Jesus specifically sent them to the Samaritans.

This was the apostles' first assignment. It will be hard enough for them to minister to their fellow Jews; Jesus knows they are not ready to handle the challenges of cross-cultural ministry. Later, they would go to Samaria and beyond. It is all in the timing. If they obstinately insisted on going to Samaria, they would have been frustrated and in rebellion, robbing them of authority and spiritual power. We must carefully listen for God's voice and know where to go, and where not to go.

In chapter 9, we will see how important lost sheep are to Jesus. The priority for this mission was the lost sheep of Israel. Even Paul, the apostle to the Gentiles, always started with the Jews. There is nothing wrong with being selective. Jesus was not being racist here; he was being obedient to the Father's clear leading. We, too, must be obedient.

Do what God tells you to do, and give freely

7 As you go, proclaim this message: 'The kingdom of heaven has come near.' 8 Heal the sick, raise the dead, cleanse those who have leprosy, drive out demons. Freely you have received; freely give.

It is not our place to invent clever new ways of doing ministry. There are many good messages the apostles could have preached: God's judgment on sin, the need for repentance, or love for God and others. But this was not the time for those messages. Here it was very simple (and probably short!): The kingdom of heaven has come near. It seems more of a teaser, designed to create interest and bring people to hear Jesus share more about the kingdom.

Preachers have a way of talking too much. It is often better to keep the message short and sweet, unless Jesus tells you to make it long and challenging! The wrong message at the wrong time can turn people off for good. It can be good to give them just enough to pique their interest so they come back for more. The truth is, these disciples did not have much knowledge to share a profound message yet, but that should not keep you from preaching! Just do not preach out of ignorance. Preach what God gives you.

At this point, more of their ministry was focused on deeds. Jesus did not waste time with something superficial. They were sent to:

- Heal the sick
- Raise the dead (how often do experienced apostles do that today?)
- Cleanse the lepers
- Drive out demons

We are in great need of *authentic* miracles. If Jesus has sent you to do miracles, he will give you the authority and power to do them.

What we have received, we are to pass on to others, without cost. Jesus had transformed their lives. He freely gave of himself, as we should do for those whom we disciple. They, in turn, should freely give what they receive.

Trust God for daily needs

⁹ "Do not get any gold or silver or copper to take with you in your belts— ¹⁰ no bag for the journey or extra shirt or sandals or a staff, for the worker is worth his keep.¹¹ Whatever town or village you enter, search there for some worthy person and stay at their house until you leave.

This was not always the case. There were times when Paul insisted on paying his way and would not receive hospitality from others. Later, Jesus would tell them to bring money for their expenses (Lk. 22:36), but here it was a no-frills ministry. They could not even bring a bag for the journey or a change of clothes. Jesus was freeing them from self-reliance and teaching them the abundance of God's provision for his workers. Again, we must carefully listen to God's instruction for each situation. There are times we would be in sin and seriously hinder our ministry if we stayed in a hotel and paid for our meals. There are other situations in which that might be necessary. The key is to hear

God's voice and be obedient. What worked on the last trip may not apply this time.

- Never be ashamed of accepting help from those you are ministering to. The worker is worth his keep. If you have ministers visiting your area, be sensitive to their needs and be ready to provide for them. There are blatant abuses by some who expect five-star hotels and fancy meals. A clean bed and a good home-cooked meal are all that is required. Do not look down on someone who comes expecting hospitality as though they are trying to use you. Perhaps they are just obeying God's instructions.

- Be careful of providing so fully for your own needs that you rob others of a blessing, or miss out on important ministry opportunities. It is usually better to minister to a family in their home than sit in a hotel room watching TV, possibly tempted by the adult channels.

- God will direct you to a "worthy" person who is ready to provide hospitality. Once you find that place, stay there for the duration. Do not move around because someone offers you better accommodations. If you are offering hospitality, be ready for the person to stay with you the whole time. They may be obeying the Lord, not trying to take advantage of you.

Know when to shake the dust off your feet

12 As you enter the home, give it your greeting. 13 If the home is deserving, let your peace rest on it; if it is not, let your peace return to you. 14 If anyone will not welcome you or listen to your words, leave that home or town and shake the dust off your feet. [15] Truly I tell you, it will be more bearable for Sodom and Gomorrah on the day of judgment than for that town.

Receiving one of Jesus' disciples is the same as receiving him, and rejecting them is rejecting Jesus (*"Whoever listens to you listens to me; whoever rejects you rejects me; but whoever rejects me rejects him who sent me"* Lk. 10:16). Jesus knew that the disciples would not always be well received. That is certainly true today as well. Do not be surprised or offended. Do not gossip about them or take it personally. Shake the dust off your feet and leave them in God's hands for judgment day. It is very serious to reject someone God has sent you!

It takes considerable sensitivity to know when to persevere in a place where you are not welcome, and when to leave. Jews would shake the dust off their feet when leaving Gentile territory, symbolically cleansing themselves. It would have been a huge insult for the disciples to shake off the dust of a Jewish town. I suspect we waste a lot of precious time and money in places that we should have left long ago.

There is spiritual power in greeting a family and offering them the peace of Christ. Here they were offering the customary Jewish "shalom"—a heartfelt desire and blessing from God for the total well-being of that family. This is a dynamic that most of us know little about: We have the tremendous privilege and opportunity to bless another family! We can let our peace—and God's blessing—rest in a place. He gives us the insight to determine whether a home is deserving, partly based on how they respond to our greeting. We can sense in the Spirit if our peace is resting there, or returning to us. If it is not deserving, let that "shalom" come back to you. You do not want to let your peace rest on an undeserving house! Do not cast your pearls before swine!

Sheep among wolves

16 "I am sending you out like sheep among wolves. Therefore be as shrewd as snakes and as innocent as doves. 17 Be on your guard; you will be handed over to the local councils and be flogged in the synagogues. 18 On my account you will be brought before governors and kings as witnesses to them and to the Gentiles. 19 But when they arrest you, do not worry about what to say or how to say it. At that time you will be given what to say, 20 for it will not be you speaking, but the Spirit of your Father speaking through you.

Jesus now moves beyond specific instructions for this first journey to the long-term implications of serving him until he returns, as mentioned in verse 23. These verses apply to us as we work to fulfill the Great Commission.

Why are we so surprised when we experience a little "persecution?" That is the norm! If there is no persecution, we are probably not being bold enough in our witness! How have we gotten the idea that everyone should be nice to us just because we are Christians? It is a rough world out there! Jesus is knowingly sending his beloved sheep into a pack of wolves. That does not mean we become wolves ourselves. We continue being sheep, but not stupid sheep. Keep the tenderness of a lamb, but be shrewd as a snake. That does not mean you descend to the world's level. Do not lose your innocence! Be as innocent as a dove! The world may laugh at you, but it is valuable in God's sight! Unfortunately, there are too many innocent sheep that are not shrewd. They get taken advantage of and devoured by the wolves. We need to find the proper balance, and that can be hard at times.

There are several specific commands here:

- Be shrewd as snakes.
- Be innocent as doves.
- Be on your guard; do not walk around blind. That does not mean fighting those who hand you over to the authorities, but we are to be alert to what is going on. We should not be caught unaware.
- Do not worry about what to say or how to say it when you are arrested. Jesus says "when" you are handed over, not "if."

There are also several "promises" here:

- You *will* be handed over to local authorities.
- You *will* be flogged by religious leaders (possibly in the church).
- You *will* be brought before governors and kings.
- You *will* be witnesses to them.
- You *will* be arrested.
- You will be given what to say by the Spirit in the time of need.

Most of us have known little of this kind of persecution, but too many of our brothers and sisters around the world are very familiar with it.

All of this is an important part of discipleship, going to the mission field (which could be your city), and putting what God has taught you into practice.

6

The Difficulty of Being a Disciple

Matthew 10:21–42

How exciting to be given the authority to heal, deliver from demons, and extend God's kingdom in this world! What a privilege to be entrusted with the commission to make disciples in every nation! But at the end of the last chapter, we already find ourselves like sheep among wolves. Jesus does not avoid hard teachings with his disciples, and this is a challenging passage. Some things are hard to interpret and others are hard to accept. I shared the cost of discipleship in the first volume in this series (Learning to Walk) to help you make an informed decision. Do you really want to be a Christian? It sounds great to walk like Jesus walked, but are you ready to pay the price? Now, in this study on leadership and the Great Commission, I assume that you have been walking with Jesus for a while. However, there is enough in the rest of this chapter to make us think twice about being part of this great mission.

In the previous chapter, I mentioned the change in Matthew 10; in verse 18, Jesus changed from specific instructions for the mission of the Twelve to prophecies about his servants' experience in the future, after his ascension, which continues for the rest of the chapter.

Divided families

[21] *"Brother will betray brother to death, and a father his child; children will rebel against their parents and have them put to death.*

Do you think you have it rough in your family? It looks like things are going to get worse.

- Are your kids rebellious? Have they gotten to the point of trying to have you put to death?
- How about your dad? Has he betrayed you?
- Your brother?

Jesus is controversial! We cannot necessarily "claim" the salvation of everyone in our families! You just may be the cause of serious division in your home! You may have to choose between your mother and Jesus, or your child and Jesus. Of course, there are promises which we like to claim:

- The Philippian jailer asked Paul and Silas: *"Sirs, what must I do to be saved?" They replied, "Believe in the Lord Jesus, and you will be saved—you and your household"* (Acts 16:30–31).
- *Start children off on the way they should go, and even when they are old they will not turn from it* (Prov. 22:6).
- *"As for me, this is my covenant with them," says the Lord. "My Spirit, who is on you, will not depart from you, and my words that I have put in your mouth will always be on your lips, on the lips of your children and on the lips of*

*their descendants—from this time on and forever," says
the Lord* (Is. 59:21).

The only New Testament "promise" for your children's salvation
is the word given to the jailer. The rest are in the context of the
Old Covenant. Of course, God can give a parent faith and a
promise for their children's salvation, but that salvation is not
guaranteed. Everyone needs to make their own decision to be
Jesus' disciple. The atmosphere of a Christian home, the example
of a church filled with God's presence and power, and the prayers
of believing parents can have a powerful impact, but
unfortunately, in these last days, we are going to see Jesus' words
fulfilled more frequently. It is easy to ignore the prophecy in
Micah 7:5–6:

> *Do not trust a neighbor;*
> *put no confidence in a friend.*
> *Even with the woman who lies in your embrace*
> *guard the words of your lips.*
> *For a son dishonors his father,*
> *a daughter rises up against her mother,*
> *a daughter-in-law against her mother-in-law—*
> *a man's enemies are the members of his own household.*

And we forget Jesus' words: *"A prophet is not without honor
except in his own town, among his relatives and in his own home."*
(Mk. 6:4).

Hated by everyone

22 *You will be hated by everyone because of me, but the one who
stands firm to the end will be saved.*

Why are we so quick to whine just because someone does not
like us? Nice as Jesus is, somehow he elicits extreme reactions in
those who oppose him, and that hatred will be passed on to us.

We are seeing more of that hatred in the world today. Just today, I saw a video that is getting thousands of "Likes," which says that the evangelical church is the American Taliban.

With the hatred and family problems, things will get so tough that it will be hard to stand firm. You may be tempted to turn back and deny Christ, just to be liked by everyone and have peace in your home and community. Standing firm may mean taking unpopular scriptural stands. You could be a regular church-goer—even a pastor—and give in to the world's pressure to be politically correct and compromise what God has clearly said.

This is a hard verse for the "once saved always saved" crowd, but Jesus said it, not me. It does not matter what prayer you prayed twenty years ago; Jesus says that it is the one *who stands firm to the end* who will be saved. If you waver and give up under the intense pressure he describes here, we can only expect God's judgment.

They will evangelize all Israel before Jesus' return?

[23] *When you are persecuted in one place, flee to another. Truly I tell you, you will not finish going through the towns of Israel before the Son of Man comes.*

There is a purpose in persecution: It gets us moving, which is evident in the book of Acts. God does not expect us to stay where we are and put up with the abuse. Jesus counsels us to get out of there! Flee to a safe place! However, once you start preaching Christ there, the persecution will probably begin again (that is what happened many times with Paul).

There is a confusing statement here about Jesus coming before they have reached every town in Israel. What are we to make of it?

- Some have suggested that before they had a chance to visit all the towns in Israel, Jesus would come after them and provide follow-up (see Luke 10:1). But the context of these verses indicates a time after the ascension.

- Others believe it speaks of the destruction of Jerusalem and the temple in AD 70 and Jesus coming back to judge them for rejecting him. However, it is a spiritualization of his second coming that seems very unlikely.

- In many of these difficult passages, the solution can be simple. Most likely, Jesus is saying that the evangelization of Israel will continue—but never be finished—until he returns. What we can affirm is that the Son of Man is coming, and we are to continue this ministry until he comes, in obedience to his Great Commission.

  o In Mark 13, where Jesus talks about the signs of the end, he says in verse 10: *And the gospel must first be preached to all nations.*

  o In Matthew 24:14, he repeats it: *And this gospel of the kingdom will be preached in the whole world as a testimony to all nations, and then the end will come.*

  o Paul says in Romans 11:25–27: *I do not want you to be ignorant of this mystery, brothers and sisters, so that you may not be conceited: Israel has experienced a hardening in part until the full number of the Gentiles has come in, and in this way all Israel will be saved. As it is written: "The deliverer will come from Zion; he will turn godlessness away from Jacob. And this is my*

> covenant with them when I take away their sins."

The mission that Jesus entrusted to his disciples here will continue until he comes again.

A servant is not above his master

[24] "The student is not above the teacher, nor a servant above his master. [25] It is enough for students to be like their teachers, and servants like their masters. If the head of the house has been called Beelzebul, how much more the members of his household!

So much for the popular teaching that Christ suffered so we would not! So much for the easy, prosperous Christian life preached by so many! You are not above Jesus! What makes you think that you, as God's servant, are better than your Master? If they hated Jesus and persecuted him, they will hate you too!

This is a variation on "walking as Jesus walked!" The student is to be like his teacher, and the servant like his master. Our aim is to be like Jesus! How great to be a member of his household! But that means if they said Jesus was of the devil, they will say the same about you.

Don't be afraid

[26] "So do not be afraid of them, for there is nothing concealed that will not be disclosed, or hidden that will not be made known. [27] What I tell you in the dark, speak in the daylight; what is whispered in your ear, proclaim from the roofs. [28] Do not be afraid of those who kill the body but cannot kill the soul. Rather, be afraid of the One who can destroy both soul and body in hell. [29] Are not two sparrows sold for a penny? Yet not one of them will fall to the ground outside your Father's care. [30] And even the

*very hairs of your head are all numbered. ³¹ So don't be afraid;
you are worth more than many sparrows.*

Are you afraid yet? Having second thoughts about serving Jesus?
Apparently, Jesus knew that his disciples were. Fear is a natural
reaction to all he has been saying, so three times in these verses
he tells them not to be afraid! And he gives three good reasons
for rejecting that fear:

- Your persecutors' hidden agendas, sin, and underhanded
  dealings will all be exposed.
- They may very well kill your body, but they cannot touch
  your soul.
- You are in God's hands. He knows you, loves you, cares
  for you, and highly values you.

There is one we should fear: God himself. He can destroy both
your body and your soul in hell. That should lead us to respect
and reverence him, and encourage us to be faithful and obedient.
Moreover, it confirms Jesus' belief in hell, a place of destruction
and eternal torment of body and soul.

Be careful with that word "destroy." Some people preach
annihilation, meaning that the devil, the demons, and all those
who reject Christ will be annihilated, or destroyed, after the great
judgment. As you know, in this life, you can destroy your own life
or other people's lives and continue living. The Bible clearly talks
of an everlasting punishment in hell; "destroy" here is not the
same as "annihilate."

Are you concealing anything that you should deal with right now?
Are there things hidden in your life that will be made known and
cause you (and your family) much pain? Better to deal with them
now. God is a god of transparency. No secrets. Don't be afraid to
proclaim what he has said, even if it gets you in big trouble!

Take some time to meditate on this beautiful truth:

- God knows you intimately.
- God loves sparrows! He knows all about them!
- He loves your dog! And your cat! He cares!
- He knows everything about you!
- He loves you! He will take care of you!

What an encouraging thought!

The danger of denying Christ

32 "Whoever acknowledges me before others, I will also acknowledge before my Father in heaven. 33 But whoever disowns me before others, I will disown before my Father in heaven.

Despite that assurance, Jesus knows that the disciples were thinking it might be better to keep quiet and stay out of trouble. You know, be a Christian, but do not announce it or irritate others by witnessing to them. Moreover, if it means saving your life, maybe even denying Christ.

No! Think twice about that! It is another blow to "eternal security:" you could be a lifelong believer, but if you disown Jesus before hostile authorities, he will disown or deny you before the Father. On the other hand, those who dare to acknowledge Jesus despite the strong possibility of persecution will be acknowledged before the Father and presumably receive a special blessing.

Jesus came to bring a sword

34 "Do not suppose that I have come to bring peace to the earth. I did not come to bring peace, but a sword. 35 For I have come to turn

> *"'a man against his father,*
> *a daughter against her mother,*
> *a daughter-in-law against her mother-in-law—*
> *³⁶   a man's enemies will be the members of his own household.'*

³⁷ "Anyone who loves their father or mother more than me is not worthy of me; anyone who loves their son or daughter more than me is not worthy of me. ³⁸ Whoever does not take up their cross and follow me is not worthy of me. ³⁹ Whoever finds their life will lose it, and whoever loses their life for my sake will find it.

Talk about turning things upside down! There are several commonly held beliefs about Christianity that we have all wrong!

- Jesus the peacemaker? *"Peace on earth, good will toward men"*? Jesus makes everything hunky dory? Wrong! He did not come to smooth things over and bring peace! He is controversial! He stirs things up! He came to bring a sword! That does not mean Jesus advocates conflict. He also said, *"Blessed are the peacemakers,"* but Jesus, the Prince of Peace, *causes* conflict.

- Jesus, the one who solves all our family issues, so we all live happily ever after? No way! We can expect the members of our own household to be our enemies! Parent/child relationships will get ugly! And be careful of loving your parents or children more than you love Jesus!

- We are all about "finding ourselves" and "fulfillment," but Jesus says that the person who is focused on self-actualization and finding their life will lose it! It is true that we are made in God's image and have great worth. The command is to love others *as we love ourselves*. God wants us to have a healthy self-image, but it is easy to make an idol out of "self." If you want to find your life and experience true self-realization, you must lose your life! Have you thought about how to lose your life for Jesus' sake?

Jesus talks several times about the person who is "worthy" of him. Are you? Jesus says that someone who loves his parents or children more than him is not worthy of him, nor is the one who does not take his cross and follow Jesus. Jesus demands our complete devotion, all our lives. Without being judgmental, would you say that most of the Christians you know are worthy of him? Is there something you need to change to be worthy of him?

This does not sound very attractive! We can expect a lot of strife if we truly are following Jesus! But there are eternal benefits.

Rewards

[40] *"Anyone who welcomes you welcomes me, and anyone who welcomes me welcomes the one who sent me.* [41] *Whoever welcomes a prophet as a prophet will receive a prophet's reward, and whoever welcomes a righteous person as a righteous person will receive a righteous person's reward.* [42] *And if anyone gives even a cup of cold water to one of these little ones who is my disciple, truly I tell you, that person will certainly not lose their reward."*

Finally, Jesus offers some encouragement. Those who welcome the disciples can expect a reward. Among all the hard hearts, there are some open hearts!

- When you welcome someone who comes in Jesus' name, you welcome Jesus, and his Father. Conversely (as in the verse I quoted earlier from Luke), if you reject Jesus' disciple, you reject him. There is tremendous loyalty in this family!

- Both prophets and righteous people can expect a reward, but you do not have to be a prophet to get that reward! Just welcome that prophet or righteous person!

- And those who show even minimal hospitality to a disciple of Jesus (like offering a glass of cold water) will be rewarded for it.

Do you really want to walk as Jesus walked?

Do you really want to be his disciple? Is this the image you were given of being sent out as an apostle? So much for a great pep talk as Jesus sends the disciples out on their first trip! Jesus was not afraid to preach the cost of discipleship. There is nothing glorious about being an apostle, or any earnest disciple of Jesus Christ. It is a hard, narrow path, but there is nothing better. There is really no other option. The alternative is hell. Are you worthy of walking it? Are you ready for all it involves? When you make disciples in obedience to Jesus' command, do you include these difficult parts?

7

The Mission of the Seventy

Luke 10:1–24

Jesus needs your help! He commanded us to make disciples of all nations, but he is short on workers! Pray for laborers for the harvest! The Holy Spirit has been working overtime preparing the hearts. Others have faithfully planted the seed. The harvest is ready. It is huge. Where are the workers?

How about you?

- Are you praying for laborers?
- Are you going out into the fields?
- Do you even know *how* to harvest? How can you tell when someone is ready to be harvested?
- Are you doing anything to prepare laborers? Like following the Master's Plan for discipleship?
- What is your circle of influence? Who are the believers you could partner with, or the unbelievers you could bring into the kingdom?

Jesus' circle of influence

Jesus' first response to this need was to call twelve disciples, appoint them as apostles, and send them out. Now he expands that group by sending out seventy additional workers. [Some manuscripts say seventy-two; either is possible. Seventy could reflect the number of Jewish elders (Exodus 24:10) while seventy-two would be a six-fold multiplication of the twelve apostles.] This is the only time the Seventy are mentioned in the New Testament.

Scripture does not give much detail about Jesus' circles of influence, but we can see:

- An inner circle of three disciples (Peter, James, and John). Together with the other nine disciples, they formed the twelve apostles.

- This group of seventy.

- A group of women who traveled with Jesus and took care of his daily needs: *After this, Jesus traveled about from one town and village to another, proclaiming the good news of the kingdom of God. The Twelve were with him, and also some women who had been cured of evil spirits and diseases: Mary (called Magdalene) from whom seven demons had come out; Joanna the wife of Chuza, the manager of Herod's household; Susanna; and many others. These women were helping to support them out of their own means* (Lk. 8:1–3).

- The 120 present in the Upper Room after his ascension, probably primarily from these groups.

- A larger group of believers (such as Nicodemus or Joseph of Arimathea) who were not publicly identified with the disciples. These may have been the 500 that saw Jesus after his resurrection.

- The multitudes who had not yet been "harvested."

We have looked at Jesus' detailed instructions as he sent out the Twelve on their first ministry trip. We will find many similarities in this passage in Luke, but some important additions as well.

[1]After this the Lord appointed seventy-two others and sent them two by two ahead of him to every town and place where he was about to go.

Appointed... not volunteered

Despite the urgent need for laborers, Jesus did not offer an open invitation for volunteers to go into the harvest. God calls, appoints, and equips those he sends. This is an important task, and great care is needed to ensure that the laborers are ready. They particularly need the authority that comes with their appointment. Are you aware of your calling? Do you believe that you have been appointed?

- Jesus works through the delegated authority of those he has appointed as leaders in his Body. Has he given you that authority?
- Are you making disciples?
- Are you carefully and faithfully appointing workers? Or do you beg for volunteers and settle for whoever you can get?
- An apostle means "to be sent." The church in Antioch *sent* Paul and Barnabas. Is your church a sending church? Does it commission workers to go out into the harvest?

Jesus had a plan!

The twelve apostles were not described as an advance team, but the Seventy were specifically sent to every town and place Jesus was about to visit, which means he had a plan! He knew where he was going next! We can be led by the Spirit and still make plans, but as Paul found out (Acts 16:6–10) and James warns (Jas. 4:13–15), those plans are always subject to change. God also has a plan to complete a task as important as the Great Commission.

- Have you sought God for a revelation of that plan?
- Where are you going?
- Is your calling to prepare the way for someone else or to have a team prepare the way for you?
- Is that function formalized? Do you even feel it is valid today?
- Could you send out some of those younger believers you are discipling to prepare the way for your ministry?
- If your role is preparing the way, are you humble in giving preference to the one who follows you?
- Have you taken the time to hear from God about where he wants you to go next?

Two by Two

The solitary worker is vulnerable:

- He is subject to more temptation, especially sexual temptation.
- He is more easily discouraged. A team can encourage each other.
- One can pray while the other is ministering.
- Two are less likely to get sidetracked.

Are we careful to follow Jesus' model today? Do you have a partner to work with in your service for Christ? It could be a husband/wife team. Pray that God would give you that person to minister with.

² He told them, "The harvest is plentiful, but the workers are few. Ask the Lord of the harvest, therefore, to send out workers into his harvest field. ³ Go! I am sending you out like lambs among wolves. ⁴ Do not take a purse or bag or sandals; and do not greet anyone on the road.

No greetings

Jesus asked the Twelve to pray; now he asks the Seventy to pray. His very next word is: "Go!" So we pray, and we go. Once again, they go as lambs—essentially to the slaughter. Like the Twelve, they cannot take a purse or a bag with them, or what most likely was a spare pair of sandals.

One additional instruction is given: Do not greet anyone on the road. Stay free of distractions and focused on the assigned task. If you are a sociable person, or in a very relational culture, that might be hard to obey, and could make you look like a snob. In the Middle Eastern Jewish culture, a greeting is usually much more than "hi." Where I live in Costa Rica, if you greet someone, you might be on your way a couple of hours later, after having a cup of coffee and sharing some good fellowship.

Are there people whom you have met on the "road" that have distracted you from the task? Do you have excess baggage you need to get rid of?

⁵ "When you enter a house, first say, 'Peace to this house.' ⁶ If someone who promotes peace is there, your peace will rest on them; if not, it will return to you. ⁷ Stay there, eating and drinking whatever they give you, for the worker deserves his wages. Do not move around from house to house. ⁸ "When you enter a town and are welcomed, eat what is offered to you.

Eat *whatever* they give you

There are two slight variations from Matthew's account:

- Jesus literally said "*a **son** of peace*," meaning someone who is inclined to peace or promotes peace. You certainly do not want to stay with someone who is not a "son of peace." The response to your greeting is a way of discerning whether you should stay there or not. Jesus wants us to stay with people of peace. That means it is usually better to stay in people's homes than in hotels, where there can be all kinds of questionable activities going on and unclean spirits in the room.

- Here, Jesus says they are to eat or drink *whatever they give you*. When you are in a very different culture or among people of very limited means, that can be challenging. However, it is rude to refuse their hospitality, and could hinder your ministry. We should be thankful for whatever is given to us. Much ministry takes place around meals, and twice Jesus commands us to eat what is offered.

⁹ Heal the sick who are there and tell them, 'The kingdom of God has come near to you.'

Heal and proclaim

The assignment was straightforward and closely resembled what Jesus told the Twelve. Healing comes first, to get their attention; then we tell them who it is that healed them. Does that describe your ministry?

The message is simple and somewhat vague—how would you feel hearing that God's kingdom had *"come near to you?"* To me, it sounds like "near," but not close enough to experience. It prepared them for Jesus' fuller teaching about the kingdom.

10 But when you enter a town and are not welcomed, go into its streets and say, 11 'Even the dust of your town we wipe from our feet as a warning to you. Yet be sure of this: The kingdom of God has come near.'12 I tell you, it will be more bearable on that day for Sodom than for that town.

Warning of judgment

Considerable power and authority are given Jesus' servants to speak judgment on unwelcoming towns. In Matthew, you could imagine the disciples sneaking out of town and shaking the dust off as they leave. Here, however, it is part of a public proclamation: the town is warned that judgment awaits them. They had a chance to experience God's kingdom—and refused it.

You may have seen Christians call down judgment on others who do not receive them. Often, they look foolish, especially as portrayed in movies. However, we should probably be bolder in following Jesus' command. How do you determine if a town has welcomed you or not? At what point do we need to pronounce judgment on them? It should not be done lightly and needs to be guided by the Holy Spirit.

13 "Woe to you, Chorazin! Woe to you, Bethsaida! For if the miracles that were performed in you had been performed in Tyre and Sidon, they would have repented long ago, sitting in sackcloth and ashes. 14 But it will be more bearable for Tyre and Sidon at the judgment than for you.15 And you, Capernaum, will you be lifted to the heavens? No, you will go down to Hades.

Miracles should lead to repentance

Capernaum was Jesus' home base in Galilee, but his presence there was not enough to have a saving impact! Jesus effectively sends them to hell, along with two other prominent Jewish cities! And Jesus cites two Gentile cities as being much more open to his ministry! He had not done miracles in Tyre and Sidon, since he was focused on the Jews at this point, but he knew they would have repented.

This response is still common today. Heavily evangelized and "Christian" areas can be practically immune to miraculous ministry, while people in developing nations who are hearing the Gospel for the first time have a heartfelt response. Jesus does not mention preaching here—it is the abundant miracles that should have brought them to repentance. But what was true then remains true today: God can raise the dead and do amazing miracles, but it still may not touch hardened hearts. Eventually, there will be a price to pay!

What about your town? Will it be lifted up to the heavens? Or go down to Hades? What about your nation?

[16] *"Whoever listens to you listens to me; whoever rejects you rejects me; but whoever rejects me rejects him who sent me."*

Jesus said this to the apostles in Matthew 10, but it was not just the Twelve; anyone whom Jesus sends out as his representative should be received as though he were Jesus himself. Jesus repeats this several times in the Gospels. It is very important! To reject Jesus is to reject the Father. You cannot accept "God" and reject his Son.

Results of the mission

17 The seventy-two returned with joy and said, "Lord, even the demons submit to us in your name."

Their experience went beyond what Jesus originally intended. They preached and healed many, but were especially impressed that even demons had to submit to them in Jesus' name. That is wonderful, but it also caused Jesus concern (perhaps that is why he had not initially mentioned it).

18 He replied, "I saw Satan fall like lightning from heaven. 19 I have given you authority to trample on snakes and scorpions and to overcome all the power of the enemy; nothing will harm you. 20 However, do not rejoice that the spirits submit to you, but rejoice that your names are written in heaven."

It is easy for the minister to get intoxicated with the power to heal and cast out demons, and lose sight of the importance of his own salvation. Jesus witnessed Satan's fall, and shudders at the thought of one of his disciples getting so prideful and carried away with spiritual power that he might rise up and try to take God's place.

Jesus has given us amazing authority: to overcome all the power of the enemy. Nothing the devil brings against us can harm us.

- Do you have some trampling to do?
- Have you been overcome by the power of the enemy? Harmed?

Grab hold of that authority and start walking in the power Jesus has given you. And rejoice that your name is written in heaven!

21 At that time Jesus, full of joy through the Holy Spirit, said, "I praise you, Father, Lord of heaven and earth, because you have hidden these things from the wise and learned, and revealed them to little children. Yes, Father, for this is what you were pleased to do.

What fills Jesus with joy

Maybe the disciples would not appreciate being called "little children," but the Father delights in hiding spiritual truth from the wise and learned of this world, and revealing it to the humble and child-like.

This is the only time the Gospels record something that brought Jesus joy. Perhaps some of it came from seeing the disciples' joy as they returned, but the main thing that delighted him was how his Father enabled humble people to grasp spiritual truth—and hid it from those who thought they were so smart.

There are only two other references to Jesus having joy:

- John 15:11: *I have told you this so that my joy may be in you and that your joy may be complete.*
- John 17:13: *I am coming to you now, but I say these things while I am still in the world, so that they may have the full measure of my joy within them.*

So we know that Jesus had joy in him, and he desires to share that joy with his disciples, but we also know that Jesus was a Man of sorrows. Maybe that is why we find so few references to him being joyful. He was carrying a lot on his shoulders!

Do you have the full measure of his joy? Do you find joy in simple things, as Jesus did?

[22] *"All things have been committed to me by my Father. No one knows who the Son is except the Father, and no one knows who the Father is except the Son and those to whom the Son chooses to reveal him."*

How to know the Father

Apparently, not just anyone can come to know the Father, and certainly not if they are from another religion and do not acknowledge Jesus. The only one who really knows Jesus is his Father! Jesus reveals the Father—and chooses whom he will reveal him to. We can pray that Jesus would reveal the Father to someone, but it is Christ's decision on who is given that privilege.

Jesus makes an all-encompassing statement here: All things have been committed to him by his Father. It reminds us of the statement in Ephesians 1:9–10, that God's purpose is to bring everything in creation together under one head, even Christ. What an amazing privilege to know Jesus—and the Father! Christ occupies an incredibly exalted position!

23 Then he turned to his disciples and said privately, "Blessed are the eyes that see what you see. 24 For I tell you that many prophets and kings wanted to see what you see but did not see it, and to hear what you hear but did not hear it."

These statements all appear to be in the context of the return of the Seventy. In case they did not realize it, they have a special blessing: to see Jesus and the manifestations of his power. Many had longed for that and never experienced it. You have a special blessing as well, in all the revelation we have received in this day, and all we have seen of God's power.

From the tenth chapters of both Matthew and Luke, we get detailed instructions on how to go about the Lord's work. The harvest is plentiful; the laborers are few. Especially few are those who walk in the authority we see here. We are part of the greatest enterprise in all of history. We have the opportunity to know the Father and his Son—those who rule the entire universe.

How closely do you follow Jesus' commands as you go about his work? Do you follow Jesus' model as you make disciples?

8

Jesus' Disciples

To walk as Jesus walked and learn how to make disciples, it makes sense to look at the twelve men who walked closest with him while he was on earth. We have studied their call and first mission. Their names appear in Matthew 10:2–4:

These are the names of the twelve apostles: first, Simon (who is called Peter) and his brother Andrew; James son of Zebedee, and his brother John; Philip and Bartholomew; Thomas and Matthew the tax collector; James son of Alphaeus, and Thaddaeus; Simon the Zealot and Judas Iscariot, who betrayed him.

Both lists (another is found in Luke 6:14–16) name Peter first, followed by his brother, the sons of Zebedee, Philip and Bartholomew, and then the rest—always ending with the traitor (Judas). What is immediately evident is the order that existed among them. What is frustrating as you dig deeper is the lack of information about them. Of course, there are many inspiring biographies of men and women who have walked with Jesus through the centuries, but our goal here is to stay close to the Scriptures. We learn a great deal about Paul's walk with Jesus, but of the Twelve, only their leader has much written about him.

Peter

Peter is like a friend to many Christians, and for good reason—we can identify with "The Rock." His name appears some 170 times in the New Testament (depending on the translation). It is interesting, considering the competition that existed with John, that John's Gospel has more references to Peter than any other Gospel. Even though many of them are not too flattering, apparently there was a closeness between them. Acts has more references than any other book (60), but Peter disappears after the Jerusalem Council in Acts 15; the rest of the book is dedicated to Paul. After Acts, Peter only appears in Paul's letter to the Galatians and in the two letters Peter authored.

We can patch together a picture of Peter—a home in Capernaum, married, impulsive—from the Scripture references. Here are some of the best-known:

- *"Lord, if it's you," Peter replied, "tell me to come to you on the water." "Come," he said. Then Peter got down out of the boat, walked on the water and came toward Jesus* (Matt. 14:28–29).

- *When Simon Peter saw this, he fell at Jesus' knees and said, "Go away from me, Lord; I am a sinful man!"* (Lk. 5:8)

- *Simon Peter answered, "You are the Messiah, the Son of the living God"* (Matt. 16:16).

- *Simon Peter answered him, "Lord, to whom shall we go? You have the words of eternal life* (Jn. 6:68).

- *Jesus turned and said to Peter, "Get behind me, Satan! You are a stumbling block to me; you do not have in mind the concerns of God, but merely human concerns"* (Matt. 16:23).

- The night of Jesus' arrest: *Then he returned to his disciples and found them sleeping. "Simon," he said to Peter, "are you asleep? Couldn't you keep watch for one hour?* (Mk. 14:37)

- *Then Simon Peter, who had a sword, drew it and struck the high priest's servant, cutting off his right ear. (The servant's name was Malchus.)* (Jn. 18:10)

- *Immediately the rooster crowed the second time. Then Peter remembered the word Jesus had spoken to him: "Before the rooster crows twice you will disown me three times." And he broke down and wept* (Mk. 14:72).

- *Peter, however, got up and ran to the tomb. Bending over, he saw the strips of linen lying by themselves, and he went away, wondering to himself what had happened* (Lk. 24:12).

- *When they had finished eating, Jesus said to Simon Peter, "Simon son of John, do you love me more than these?" "Yes, Lord," he said, "you know that I love you." Jesus said, "Feed my lambs"* (Jn. 21:15).

- On Pentecost: *Then Peter stood up with the Eleven, raised his voice and addressed the crowd: "Fellow Jews and all of you who live in Jerusalem, let me explain this to you; listen carefully to what I say* (Acts 2:14).

- *Then Peter said, "Silver or gold I do not have, but what I do have I give you. In the name of Jesus Christ of Nazareth, walk"* (Acts 3:6).

- *As a result, people brought the sick into the streets and laid them on beds and mats so that at least Peter's shadow might fall on some of them as he passed by* (Acts 5:15).

- *Suddenly an angel of the Lord appeared and a light shone in the cell. He struck Peter on the side and woke him up. "Quick, get up!" he said, and the chains fell off Peter's wrists* (Acts 12:7).

- *When Cephas came to Antioch, I opposed him to his face, because he stood condemned. For before certain men came from James, he used to eat with the Gentiles. But when they arrived, he began to draw back and separate himself from the Gentiles because he was afraid of those who belonged to the circumcision group. The other Jews joined him in his hypocrisy, so that by their hypocrisy even Barnabas was led astray* (Gal. 2:11–13).

If you have never studied Peter's life, look up the context of each of these references, and write down what you learn about him. What can you identify with most? What do you see as his strengths and weaknesses?

Peter's two letters are full of wisdom; I have written a book about them, Letters from the Rock.

John and James

After Peter, John is mentioned most frequently (but only 34 times), although John wrote far more than Peter: his Gospel, three letters, and Revelation. Based on Scriptures referring to John, he has been called rash, impetuous, aggressive, reckless, zealous, passionate, and ambitious:

- *"Teacher," said John, "we saw someone driving out demons in your name and we told him to stop, because he was not one of us." "Do not stop him," Jesus said* (Mark 9:38–39).

- *As the time approached for him to be taken up to heaven, Jesus resolutely set out for Jerusalem. And he sent messengers on ahead, who went into a Samaritan village to get things ready for him; but the people there did not welcome him, because he was heading for Jerusalem. When the disciples James and John saw this, they asked, "Lord, do you want us to call fire down from heaven to destroy them?"* (Lk. 9:51–54)

In his Gospel, John usually refers to himself as the "one whom Jesus loved," and the enduring picture is of him leaning on Jesus' chest at the Last Supper. He seemed to mellow significantly in later years and was probably the last apostle to die.

James was John's older brother and is often mentioned together with him. Jesus called them "sons of thunder," which probably says something about their personalities. Their mother, Salome, was one of the women who followed Jesus to care for his daily needs. James was the first apostle martyred (Acts 12:2). The brothers, along with Peter, made up Jesus' inner circle.

Andrew

The first apostle to follow Jesus, Andrew was Peter's brother and introduced him to Jesus. He had been a disciple of John the Baptist and, along with Peter, was called to be a fisher of men. Andrew noticed the loaves and fish available to feed the multitude, but did not have the faith to see how Jesus could use them:

Another of his disciples, Andrew, Simon Peter's brother, spoke up, "Here is a boy with five small barley loaves and two small fish, but how far will they go among so many?" (John 6:8–9)

Andrew, Peter, the sons of Zebedee, and Philip were all from Bethsaida and were all fishermen.

Bartholomew (Nathanael)

Bartholomew was also called Nathanael. He was from Cana in Galilee; it is very possible that the couple at the wedding in Cana was family or friends of Bartholomew.

More is written about his call to follow Jesus than about any other disciple:

The next day Jesus decided to leave for Galilee. Finding Philip, he said to him, "Follow me." Philip, like Andrew and Peter, was from the town of Bethsaida. Philip found Nathanael and told him, "We have found the one Moses wrote about in the Law, and about whom the prophets also wrote—Jesus of Nazareth, the son of Joseph." "Nazareth! Can anything good come from there?" Nathanael asked. Come and see," said Philip. When Jesus saw Nathanael approaching, he said of him, "Here truly is an Israelite in whom there is no deceit." "How do you know me?" Nathanael asked. Jesus answered, "I saw you while you were still under the fig tree before Philip called you." Then Nathanael declared, "Rabbi, you are the Son of God; you are the king of Israel." Jesus said, "You believe because I told you I saw you under the fig tree. You will see greater things than that." He then added, "Very truly I tell you, you will see 'heaven open, and the angels of God ascending and descending on' the Son of Man" (Jn. 1:43–51).

Beyond that, nothing is known about him.

Philip

In addition to Philip's call and role in bringing Nathanael to Jesus, there are these three references:

- *The Jewish Passover Festival was near. When Jesus looked up and saw a great crowd coming toward him, he said to Philip, "Where shall we buy bread for these people to eat?" He asked this only to test him, for he already had in mind what he was going to do* (Jn. 6:4–6).

- *Now there were some Greeks among those who went up to worship at the festival. They came to Philip, who was from Bethsaida in Galilee, with a request. "Sir," they said, "we would like to see Jesus." Philip went to tell Andrew; Andrew and Philip in turn told Jesus* (Jn. 12:20–22). Philip had a Greek name and probably spoke Greek. He may have served as a link to that community. His going to Andrew may reflect order among the apostles; for some reason, he may not have felt comfortable going to Jesus alone.

- *Philip said, "Lord, show us the Father and that will be enough for us." Jesus answered: "Don't you know me, Philip, even after I have been among you such a long time? Anyone who has seen me has seen the Father. How can you say, 'Show us the Father'?* (Jn. 14:8–9)

Philip the apostle is not to be confused with Philip the evangelist in the book of Acts.

Judas Iscariot

Everyone knows Judas Iscariot because he betrayed Jesus. He was the group's treasurer, and his weakness for money may have led to his downfall:

- *Then Satan entered Judas, called Iscariot, one of the Twelve* (Lk. 22:3).

- *When Judas, who had betrayed him, saw that Jesus was condemned, he was seized with remorse and returned the thirty pieces of silver to the chief priests and the elders. "I have sinned," he said, "for I have betrayed innocent blood." "What is that to us?" they replied. "That's your responsibility." So Judas threw the money into the temple and left. Then he went away and hanged himself* (Matt. 27:3–5).

Matthew

Also called Levi, Matthew was a publican, or tax collector. Better educated than most of the apostles, he wrote the first Gospel. Matthew was the son of Alphaeus.

After this, Jesus went out and saw a tax collector by the name of Levi sitting at his tax booth. "Follow me," Jesus said to him, and Levi got up, left everything and followed him. Then Levi held a great banquet for Jesus at his house, and a large crowd of tax collectors and others were eating with them. But the Pharisees and the teachers of the law who belonged to their sect complained to his disciples, "Why do you eat and drink with tax collectors and sinners?" Jesus answered them, "It is not the healthy who need a doctor, but the sick. (Lk. 5:27–31)

Thomas (Aramaic), also called Didymus (Greek)

Both names mean twin, although we have no knowledge of his twin. Best known for his doubts, the three references we have to him do not leave a very favorable impression.

When Jesus went to raise Lazarus from the dead, Thomas knew things were already dangerous in Judah, and he did not seem to have much faith:

Then Thomas (also known as Didymus) said to the rest of the disciples, "Let us also go, that we may die with him" (Jn. 11:16).

In the Upper Room, Thomas still did not seem too bright:

You know the way to the place where I am going." Thomas said to him, "Lord, we don't know where you are going, so how can we know the way?" Jesus answered, "I am the way and the truth and the life. No one comes to the Father except through me (John 14:4-6).

Thomas is most famous for his doubts after the resurrection:

Now Thomas (also known as Didymus), one of the Twelve, was not with the disciples when Jesus came. So the other disciples told him, "We have seen the Lord!" But he said to them, "Unless I see the nail marks in his hands and put my finger where the nails were, and put my hand into his side, I will not believe."

A week later his disciples were in the house again, and Thomas was with them. Though the doors were locked, Jesus came and stood among them and said, "Peace be with you!" Then he said to Thomas, "Put your finger here; see my hands. Reach out your hand and put it into my side. Stop doubting and believe."

Thomas said to him, "My Lord and my God!"

Then Jesus told him, "Because you have seen me, you have believed; blessed are those who have not seen and yet have believed" (John 20:24-29).

There are traditions about the later ministry and deaths of most of these apostles—many are questionable in their authenticity.

One of the most clearly supported regards Thomas; he was probably responsible for bringing the Gospel to India.

The last three

James, often called "The Lesser" to differentiate him from James the son of Zebedee, was a son of Alphaeus. He may have been Matthew's brother, since both were sons of Alphaeus.

Thaddeus was the second Judas, also called Jude (but not the author of the biblical letter from Jude). Luke identifies him as the son of James. He is only mentioned once and is primarily known for *not* being Judas Iscariot:

Then Judas (not Judas Iscariot) said, "But, Lord, why do you intend to show yourself to us and not to the world?" (Jn. 14:22)

Much conjecture has swirled around Simon the Zealot (or the Canaanite). His name may have described him as a patriot of Israel and political radical, or it could just mean "zealous." Nothing else is known about him.

So what do we learn?

To me, the most glaring takeaway is the possibility of walking faithfully and intimately with Jesus, yet remaining in relative obscurity. Jesus personally chose each of these twelve men after an intensive night of prayer with his Father. They all were sent out with the authority to heal, cast out demons, and preach the kingdom, and they did that. However, when the Gospels were written, there was practically nothing to write about the majority of them.

Many of us would probably like to be a Peter: bold, walking on water, a man's man. Or at least be part of Jesus' inner circle, perhaps a "disciple whom Jesus loved" like John. Does that mean he loved John more than the others? I do not think so, but they did have a special relationship.

Unfortunately, we can't all be part of the inner circle. There is obvious order among these disciples, and if God has chosen me to be a James the Lesser, I need to accept that. The focus is on the One I am walking with and serving, not me.

Hopefully, we can have stronger faith than Thomas and certainly not be an instrument of the devil, like Judas. But the devil messed with Peter as well, prompting Jesus to rebuke him: *"Get behind me, Satan."*

These are important things to remember as we disciple others. Walking with Jesus does not always mean we will be the center of attention. It does not necessarily mean we will have a great ministry. What most impresses me is that each of these men got to be with Jesus, and that is my primary desire as I seek to walk closely with him, and like him.

9

Leading as Jesus Led

To walk as Jesus walked involves leadership. Jesus was a leader; in fact, he was the greatest leader who ever walked this earth. We want to lead as Jesus led, and make disciples as he made disciples. We have a lot to learn from him. If we walk as he walked, we will be great leaders and will make great disciples.

We have looked at those he called, appointed, and sent out as apostles. So far, they had limited responsibilities: heal the sick, deliver the demonized, and preach the kingdom. That is a great start, but any good pastor will tell you that there is more to leadership. Peter stood out as a natural leader. Jesus recognized and encouraged that leadership, but the very qualities God would powerfully use also caused Jesus headaches. Peter had many lessons to learn along the way. Natural leaders are probably more mistake-prone than the quiet person who stays in the background.

From Jesus' teachings and example, what can we learn about leadership and the kind of disciple we want to form?

Do for us whatever we ask! Matthew 20:20–28

²⁰ Then the mother of Zebedee's sons came to Jesus with her sons and, kneeling down, asked a favor of him.

Her request reflects every mother's desire for her son's success. It is hard to say whether James and John put her up to this, or if she encouraged them to approach Jesus. Mark's version (Mk. 10:35–45) does not mention her, but exposes the sons' arrogance: *"Teacher," they said, "we want you to do for us whatever we ask."*

Have you ever come to the Lord like that? It is bold, but Jesus does not automatically condemn their desire for a favor, for him to do *"whatever we ask,"* as being out of place. He is willing to hear them out. There probably are times when we amuse him.

²¹ "What is it you want?" he asked.

She said, "Grant that one of these two sons of mine may sit at your right and the other at your left in your kingdom."

Instead of trusting Jesus to decide who should sit at his right and left—and accepting whoever it might be—they hope he will do what they ask. After all, John was the "beloved disciple" (Jn. 13:23; 21:7). There was often competition between him and Peter, and part of this may have been John pre-empting any attempt by Peter to gain this position.

It is human nature to want to be first, at least fallen human nature. We want the best places, most influence, and most money. Would you be tempted to ask Jesus this favor if you had been one of the Twelve? How would you have felt if you were Peter? How do you think Jesus felt?

²² "You don't know what you are asking," Jesus said to them. "Can you drink the cup I am going to drink?"

"We can," they answered.

Jesus was a master at handling awkward situations. He does not rebuke them, but responds with a question. Learn how to use questions as Jesus did! Do not be too quick to jump on people! The brothers have no clue what is involved in being that close to Jesus. Leadership looks glamorous, but there is far more involved than glamor. Ask any pastor or government leader.

Have you ever asked Jesus for something that would probably elicit the same response? *"You don't know what you are asking."* James and John were a little too quick to affirm that they could drink the cup Jesus was going to drink. They did not realize what that meant, but in our rush to the top, we can make many promises and declarations that we do not know how to keep, or have any intention of keeping.

23 Jesus said to them, "You will indeed drink from my cup, but to sit at my right or left is not for me to grant. These places belong to those for whom they have been prepared by my Father."

Jesus very graciously turns them down. Part of leadership is accepting the authority of those over you. Jesus does not say he would go to his Father and speak on behalf of James and John. He does not even affirm that he would like to have them sitting at his side. It is fascinating to know that the Father has prepared those places and chosen two people who will sit at Jesus' side. We could try to guess who they would be, but it is best to leave that kind of speculation alone and let God be God.

24 When the ten heard about this, they were indignant with the two brothers.

We can easily understand their indignation, but it provides a great teaching opportunity for Jesus.

Two kinds of leadership

25 Jesus called them together and said, "You know that the rulers of the Gentiles lord it over them, and their high officials exercise authority over them.

There are two very distinct kinds of leadership. First, worldly leaders, who:

- Lord it over those who are under them.
- See leadership as an opportunity to exert authority (NLT: *flaunt their authority*), if necessary, using force to get compliance.

26 Not so with you. Instead, whoever wants to become great among you must be your servant, 27 and whoever wants to be first must be your slave— 28 just as the Son of Man did not come to be served, but to serve, and to give his life as a ransom for many."

The second kind of leadership is like the Son of Man's:

- It does not look to the world for role models. The first step toward authentic leadership is to discard any thought of lording it over others.

- The key word is "servant."
    - If you want to become great, if you have the heart of James and John to seek a high position in the kingdom, get busy looking for every opportunity to serve.
    - Put aside your rights and become a voluntary slave—of Jesus, but also in service to other people.
    - Resist any inclination to have others wait on you and serve you. Study Jesus' example of servanthood.

- The leader is ready to lay down his life for those he is serving. No cost is too great. Not many leaders are ready to do that.

It is easy for a leader to fall into the demanding attitude of "do for us whatever we ask." It starts with the demands we place on those under us, but we can even arrogantly assume that attitude with God. Fight it!

Foot washing: John 13:13–17

On the night of his betrayal and arrest, just before the sharing of the first Lord's Supper, Jesus provided us with a powerful visual of servanthood. It was usually the task of the household servant or slave to wash the dusty, sandal-clad feet of visitors. It was not a pleasant job; no one would rush to perform it. Jesus shocks his disciples by getting up from the table to wash their feet. Characteristically, Peter protests. He would rather be washing Jesus' feet, but Jesus insists that Peter humble himself and allow his Lord to serve him in this manner.

13 "You call me 'Teacher' and 'Lord,' and rightly so, for that is what I am.

Jesus never denies his position. Servanthood and humility have nothing to do with pretending your position is not important, but you do not flaunt it or use it for your own benefit. You do not demand that people bow down to you or call you by a particular title. Jesus avoided titles. He accepted being called Teacher and Lord, but the implication of that position is far different than what we might expect.

14 Now that I, your Lord and Teacher, have washed your feet, you also should wash one another's feet. 15 I have set you an example that you should do as I have done for you.

There has been considerable discussion about foot washing. Do we need to actually follow Jesus' example, or simply find other ways to humble ourselves and be servants? I believe both are important. Jesus explicitly says we should do what he did. Servanthood goes much deeper than an occasional foot washing, but just like the Lord's Supper is a great reminder of Jesus' sacrifice, foot washing reminds us of the need to humbly serve others.

How long has it been since there has been a foot washing in your church? Churches that do practice it often limit it to Holy Week. Why not surprise people and do it a few times a year? What are some other ways you can "wash feet" this coming week?

16 Very truly I tell you, no servant is greater than his master, nor is a messenger greater than the one who sent him.17 Now that you know these things, you will be blessed if you do them.

Jesus already stated this in connection with them expecting persecution (Matt. 10:24). How dare we think that as leaders in his Body we are above menial, humiliating tasks like foot washing!

Who is the greatest? Luke 22:24–30

Do you compare yourself with others? Were you a teacher's pet? Or maybe some relative's favorite? Have you ever jockeyed for position in church or on the job? Any of those can lead to all kinds of problems.

Not surprisingly, Jesus' disciples were not immune from power plays. Tragically, this dispute occurred during the Last Supper, right after the powerful example of foot washing. They had not gotten the message when the issue arose after James' and John's request.

²⁴ A dispute also arose among them as to which of them was considered to be greatest. ²⁵ Jesus said to them, "The kings of the Gentiles lord it over them; and those who exercise authority over them call themselves Benefactors. ²⁶ But you are not to be like that. Instead, the greatest among you should be like the youngest, and the one who rules like the one who serves.

There is the "benevolent dictator." There have been many in world history. People may put up with their tyranny because they get taken care of. Some pastors and Christian leaders have assumed that stance as well, but anything that smacks of authoritarianism is out of place in the church. That is a hard word for many pastors who feel they can rule their church with an iron fist.

Here, Jesus introduces the aspect of age, as well as the attitude of servanthood. Typically, young people are viewed as being inexperienced and immature. This is not a call to place young people in leadership, although at times that can be appropriate. Instead, it is a call to not only avoid the authoritarianism that can accompany age, but to be like the "youngest," or, as we will see in a moment, like a child, voluntarily humbling yourself and taking a lower position. From that place, we have the heart to lead as Jesus led.

²⁷ For who is greater, the one who is at the table or the one who serves? Is it not the one who is at the table? But I am among you as one who serves.

In the world, it is obvious that the person being waited on is more important than the one serving them. Not so in the kingdom. The Christian—and especially the leader—delights in taking the lowest place, preferring to serve others over being served himself.

Which brings you more satisfaction? Having others wait on you hand and foot? Or jumping at every opportunity to serve someone else?

28 You are those who have stood by me in my trials. 29 And I confer on you a kingdom, just as my Father conferred one on me, 30 so that you may eat and drink at my table in my kingdom and sit on thrones, judging the twelve tribes of Israel.

Servanthood is not incompatible with power or authority. Jesus—the greatest servant of all—had the kingdom of heaven conferred on him, and he passes that kingdom on to his disciples! Yes, they may wait tables here on earth, but in heaven they will be eating and drinking at the Lord's table and sitting on thrones as judges!

Are you willing to humble yourself now and trust God to lift you up in the future—if he wants to?

The least is the greatest: Luke 9:46—48

Discussions of who would be greatest were not limited to the Upper Room; on another occasion, Jesus provided this perspective on greatness:

46 An argument started among the disciples as to which of them would be the greatest. 47 Jesus, knowing their thoughts, took a little child and had him stand beside him. 48 Then he said to them, "Whoever welcomes this little child in my name welcomes me; and whoever welcomes me welcomes the one who sent me. For it is the one who is least among you all who is the greatest."

Children in Jesus' day had no rights and certainly would not be viewed as great in the kingdom. The disciples reflected that attitude as they tried to keep children away from Jesus (Mk.

10:13–14, also Matt. 19:13–14 and Lk. 18:15–16), and Jesus was indignant with them. Kingdom values are often the opposite of worldly values. Unfortunately, our understanding of greatness tends to be very worldly.

What words come to your mind to describe someone great? How does that compare with Jesus' definition? What people have been great in the world's eyes? Who can you think of that you would say is great in Jesus' eyes?

You must become like a child: Matthew 18:3–7

Jesus has given various perspectives on leadership and greatness. Now he takes this issue of childlikeness one dramatic step further: you cannot even enter the kingdom unless you become like a child:

³ And he said: "Truly I tell you, unless you change and become like little children, you will never enter the kingdom of heaven. ⁴ Therefore, whoever takes the lowly position of this child is the greatest in the kingdom of heaven. ⁵ And whoever welcomes one such child in my name welcomes me.

It is one thing to adopt a servant's attitude and humble yourself, but Jesus requires much more, not just of leaders, but of anyone in his kingdom! We must change and become like little children.

⁶ "If anyone causes one of these little ones—those who believe in me—to stumble, it would be better for them to have a large millstone hung around their neck and to be drowned in the depths of the sea. ⁷ Woe to the world because of the things that cause people to stumble! Such things must come, but woe to the person through whom they come!

This is a stern warning to leaders. If you, in your position as pastor or Christian leader, cause a simple, humble believer to stumble, you face severe judgment. Those are powerful words! How many believers, in their quest for position, influence, and power, have caused younger believers to stumble?

Jesus has a sobering word for the idealist: there will be stumbling blocks! People will do mean things to you that will cause you to stumble! Be careful of being overly hard on yourself if someone has done that—but be honest about your responsibility in the situation.

- Is there anything you are doing right now that is causing people to stumble?
- Are you running roughshod over "little ones" in your quest for the top?
- Are you like James and John, seeking position and influence? Or like their mother, trying to manipulate the situation for the benefit of someone close to you?
- How are you demonstrating a servant's heart?

Whether at home, at work, or in the church, are you leading as Jesus led? What kind of disciples are you making? What example do you offer them?

10

A Pastor Like Jesus

John 10:1–21

Jesus established five offices in the church: apostle, prophet, evangelist, pastor, and teacher (Eph. 4:11). Apostles, prophets, and evangelists are in the vanguard of completing the Great Commission, but at times, in their zeal to plant churches and gain many new believers for the kingdom, they may ignore the important offices of pastor and teacher, and end up losing many of the sheep who have accepted Christ. We have seen that the Commission is to make disciples, not converts. It is possible to build a large church that experiences many signs and wonders, but to establish a true disciple-making body of Christ, the pastoral ministry is essential. When the apostle who plants a church fails to install a pastor with Jesus' heart, he may lose many sheep and leave the door open for the devil.

Thieves and robbers

[1] *"Very truly I tell you Pharisees, anyone who does not enter the sheep pen by the gate, but climbs in by some other way, is a thief and a robber.*

There is order in God's kingdom. Not just anyone can decide they want to pastor a church. There is only one door, or gate, by which a pastor can enter to care for the sheep. Jesus knows that just as there are many false prophets in the church, there are many thieves and robbers disguised as pastors, and he is very concerned about it.

A thief comes to steal. He does not think about the sheep and their well-being; he only thinks about himself and how he can take advantage of others. He *sneaks over the wall* (NLT). He has no respect for boundaries or authority.

Pastor, be careful of whom you let teach and lead in your church. Establish clearly defined "gates" to enter the church and the ministry, and do whatever is necessary to protect your flock from robbers. A thief may already be in your sheep pen, and it is up to you to take authority in Jesus' name to remove him.

The pastor calls his sheep by name

[2] The one who enters by the gate is the shepherd of the sheep.[3] The gatekeeper opens the gate for him, and the sheep listen to his voice. He calls his own sheep by name and leads them out.

There are many flocks in Jesus' sheepfold. He knows the pastors he has called to care for his sheep. Yes, the sheep belong to Jesus, the owner of the sheep pen, but he entrusts them to the pastor to feed and watch over them. A true pastor knows the names of his sheep and takes the initiative in seeking them out and calling them by name. He loves them and wants to take care of them. A lamb does not wander from one flock to another looking for a pastor he likes; the lamb waits for his pastor to call him out.

What does that mean for churches and sheep today? Could it be the pastor's responsibility to visit people, evangelize, and call someone to be part of his flock? Or, if he grew up in the church and was discipled there, would he already know the sheep and be placed in the position of pastor by someone in authority over the church? There are many backslidden sheep who are fed up with the sheep pen; they waited for their pastor, but he never showed up, and they have gone elsewhere to seek greener pastures.

⁴ When he has brought out all his own, he goes on ahead of them, and his sheep follow him because they know his voice.

The pastor does not start his ministry until he has brought out all his sheep. He doesn't want to miss or lose even one. The Lord reveals to him how many there are, and he knows when he has them all. If the pastor is trained in his home congregation, part of his formation could be seeking the Lord to know who his sheep are and establishing a relationship with them. They could be people he discipled. Then he is sent out and commissioned by the church to leave that sheep pen and plant a new church. How different from the usual concept of pastoring! The pastor has a great responsibility; the sheep need only to listen for his voice and follow him. The foundation of the ministry is the pastor/sheep relationship, just like the relationship of Jesus and his disciples.

The pastor needs direction; he needs to know where to go. The Lord may use a prophet to provide that direction, just as Paul and Barnabas were set apart (Acts 13:2). It is clear that the pastor has authority, and the sheep trust him and follow him. He has a great responsibility: never to deceive the sheep or lead them into danger. The problem could be the rebellious sheep who does not want to stay with the rest of the flock or follow the pastor, and may distract the pastor from caring for the others.

⁵ But they will never follow a stranger; in fact, they will run away from him because they do not recognize a stranger's voice."

God has given sheep the ability to recognize their pastor's voice and follow only him. If their discernment is functioning correctly, they will never follow a stranger; they will flee from him. It is a sense God gives us (and animals) for our well-being and protection. The sheep are safest when this entire process takes place within the authority of a local body, with godly covering functioning according to Jesus' plan. This is very different from the usual concept of pastoring! Do you think it is closer to Jesus' heart and potentially healthier for the sheep?

Jesus is the gate

⁶ Jesus used this figure of speech, but the Pharisees did not understand what he was telling them.

The Pharisees—like Jesus' own disciples many times—did not understand what Jesus meant, but he graciously explained the parable:

⁷ Therefore Jesus said again, "Very truly I tell you, I am the gate for the sheep.

Jesus is the way, the truth, and the life; he is the only gate for the sheep. There is no other way into the kingdom of heaven. Just like the way is a person, the gate is a person, and a personal relationship with Christ. He knows when they come into the sheep pen, when they leave, and with whom.

⁸ All who have come before me are thieves and robbers, but the sheep have not listened to them.

This is a bold statement. Does it mean there were no good priests or leaders among the Jews who truly took care of the people? It places a high expectation on pastors in the kingdom.

⁹ I am the gate; whoever enters through me will be saved. They will come in and go out, and find pasture.

The type of leadership Jesus models involves freedom and feeding. Within the limits of his flock, there is freedom. Yes, we are Christ's servants and must submit to him, but something is wrong if there is no freedom in a church or the sheep feel controlled like slaves. The sheep should find rest, safety, and the spiritual food they need. The Bible calls us to submit to the pastor and elders, but they should never control the sheep like tyrants:

Shepherd and guide and protect the flock of God among you, exercising oversight not under compulsion, but voluntarily, according to the will of God; and not [motivated] for shameful gain, but with wholehearted enthusiasm; not lording it over those assigned to your care [do not be arrogant or overbearing], but be examples [of Christian living] to the flock [set a pattern of integrity for your congregation] (1 Pet. 5:2–3, AMP).

The good pastor gives abundant life

¹⁰ The thief comes only to steal and kill and destroy; I have come that they may have life, and have it to the full.

The pastor must watch for the thief. Too many sheep have lost their families and ministries; too many dreams—and even people—have died because they fell into the devil's trap. He wants to destroy you, and the battle is fierce. If you feel death and are losing something precious to you, wake up! If they are asking for money, be careful. The thief is attacking you. You must resist him.

You should feel life in a church. The abundant life should be evident in the leaders—the abundant life Jesus desires for you, which is only available in a relationship with him. When a church seems dead, chances are the thief has already taken over.

[11] *"I am the good shepherd. The good shepherd lays down his life for the sheep. [12] The hired hand is not the shepherd and does not own the sheep. So when he sees the wolf coming, he abandons the sheep and runs away. Then the wolf attacks the flock and scatters it. [13] The man runs away because he is a hired hand and cares nothing for the sheep.*

The wolf and the hired hand

Jesus already spoke about the difference between a true pastor and a thief. Now he presents two more threats: the wolf and the hired hand who is not really a pastor at all. For him, it is just a job. Maybe someone pressured him to pastor, or he may see the pastorate as a comfortable position from which he can control and take advantage of the sheep and become wealthy. He thinks of only one person: himself. He does not care about the sheep. When there are problems in the church, he takes off. This person may be a good preacher and look like a man of God, but God did not call him and he is not a pastor.

The sheep should have the discernment to know that the wolf does not talk like a pastor and will not follow him. However, they are sheep, easily deceived by a charismatic personality, great messages, and promises of blessings and prosperity.

It would seem that Jesus, with his power and authority, could simply protect his beloved flock, kill the wolf, and throw out the hired hand. But he allows them, perhaps to test and strengthen us. Anyone can see that a wolf comes to kill, but most wolves are disguised as sheep. The church is full of them. One sure sign of the wolf's work is scattered sheep. His attacks almost always result in divisions, wounded sheep, and resentful believers who leave the church and possibly the Lord.

The pastor knows his sheep

14 "I am the good shepherd; I know my sheep and my sheep know me—15 just as the Father knows me and I know the Father—and I lay down my life for the sheep.

What Jesus says is very impressive! The intimate relationship that exists between the Father and the Son also exists between us and Jesus. That has significant implications for ministry. The pastor must truly know his sheep, and they have to know him. That is the relationship we have with Jesus, and the relationship Christ wants between his pastors and their flocks. They should spend time together and share their lives. The commitment and self-sacrifice are so great that a pastor is ready to lay down his life for the sheep.

Other sheep pens

16 I have other sheep that are not of this sheep pen. I must bring them also. They too will listen to my voice, and there shall be one flock and one shepherd.

Jesus is talking about the Gentiles; God's plan is to unite all his sheep in one flock under Jesus' authority.

17 The reason my Father loves me is that I lay down my life—only to take it up again. 18 No one takes it from me, but I lay it down of my own accord. I have authority to lay it down and authority to take it up again. This command I received from my Father."

The Father is pleased with the pastor who lays down his life for his sheep, but Jesus has divine power: after giving up his life on the cross, he took it up again.

This is an answer for those who hate Jews because they "killed Jesus." No, Jesus laid down his life of his own volition. He voluntarily came to this world, knowing he was going to die. No one can take Jesus' life. Unlike us, he is God and has the authority to lay his life down and to take it up again. No man can do that.

¹⁹ The Jews who heard these words were again divided. ²⁰ Many of them said, "He is demon-possessed and raving mad. Why listen to him?"

²¹ But others said, "These are not the sayings of a man possessed by a demon. Can a demon open the eyes of the blind?"

They lost the blessing of entering into eternal life and being part of the sheep pen because they fixated on Jesus' controversial words about his life and death. Jesus is always controversial when we analyze what he said. The Jews knew that no mere man has that control over his life, but Jesus' miracles confirmed that he must be from God.

Jesus repeats that a true pastor lays down his life for his sheep: Luke 15:1–7

This is another parable that clearly shows the importance of each sheep:

¹Now the tax collectors and sinners were all gathering around to hear Jesus. ² But the Pharisees and the teachers of the law muttered, "This man welcomes sinners and eats with them."

Here, the context is the disdain of the religious leaders for the "sinners" who followed Jesus.

³ Then Jesus told them this parable: ⁴"Suppose one of you has a hundred sheep and loses one of them. Doesn't he leave the ninety-nine in the open country and go after the lost sheep until he finds it? ⁵ And when he finds it, he joyfully puts it on his shoulders⁶ and goes home. Then he calls his friends and neighbors together and says, 'Rejoice with me; I have found my lost sheep.' [7] I tell you that in the same way there will be more rejoicing in heaven over one sinner who repents than over ninety-nine righteous persons who do not need to repent.

It reminds us of the prodigal son and his older brother's reaction (Lk. 15:25–32). This is one sheep out of one hundred, one percent. It is not unusual for 10 or 25% of a church to be lost in the world. Many pastors do not have the time or the interest to seek out those lost sheep; they may even dismiss them as sinners who do not take the gospel seriously. However, Jesus' example is that each sheep is valuable; he does not want to lose even one.

I have also seen pastors abandon the ninety-nine to dedicate all their time to the rebellious and backslidden sheep. That is not appropriate either.

Ezekiel 34

The best-known passage about pastors in the Old Testament, which every Jew was familiar with, is in Ezekiel 34. It is an important glimpse of God's heart about his pastors and their responsibilities.

[1] The word of the Lord came to me: [2] "Son of man, prophesy against the shepherds of Israel; prophesy and say to them: 'This is what the Sovereign Lord says: Woe to you shepherds of Israel who only take care of yourselves! Should not shepherds take care of the flock? [3] You eat the curds, clothe yourselves with the wool and slaughter the choice animals, but you do not take care of the flock. [4] You have not strengthened the weak or healed the sick or bound up the injured. You have not brought back the strays or searched for the lost. You have ruled them harshly and brutally. [5] So they were scattered because there was no shepherd, and when they were scattered they became food for all the wild animals. [6] My sheep wandered over all the mountains

*and on every high hill. They were scattered over the whole earth,
and no one searched or looked for them.*

God's complaints against the pastors

- They care only for themselves and not the flock.
- They abuse and rob the flock, taking the milk, using their
  wool, and killing the choice animals.
- They do not strengthen the weak sheep.
- They do not take care of the sick sheep.
- They do not bind up the wounded sheep.
- They do not bring back the strays or search for the lost.
- They rule over the sheep harshly and brutally.

As a result:

- The sheep are scattered.
- They are at the mercy of wild animals.
- They wander over mountains and on every high hill.
- There is no one to take care of them; they are vulnerable.

The Lord does not blame the sheep for being rebellious or
wandering away; part of being a sheep is getting hurt and being
weak at times. The Lord blames the pastors and makes them
responsible for the sheep's misery.

God's judgment on those pastors

[7] *"'Therefore, you shepherds, hear the word of the Lord:* [8] *As
surely as I live, declares the Sovereign Lord, because my flock
lacks a shepherd and so has been plundered and has become food
for all the wild animals, and because my shepherds did not search
for my flock but cared for themselves rather than for my
flock,* [9] *therefore, you shepherds, hear the word of
the Lord:* [10] *This is what the Sovereign Lord says: I am against the
shepherds and will hold them accountable for my flock. I will*

remove them from tending the flock so that the shepherds can no longer feed themselves. I will rescue my flock from their mouths, and it will no longer be food for them.

When a pastor does not fulfill his God-given call, the Lord:

- Is against him.
- Holds him accountable for the flock.
- Removes him from tending the flock.
- Afflicts him so he can no longer feed himself.
- Rescues the flock from his mouth.

How God pastors his sheep

[11] *"'For this is what the Sovereign Lord says: I myself will search for my sheep and look after them. [12] As a shepherd looks after his scattered flock when he is with them, so will I look after my sheep. I will rescue them from all the places where they were scattered on a day of clouds and darkness. [13] I will bring them out from the nations and gather them from the countries, and I will bring them into their own land. I will pasture them on the mountains of Israel, in the ravines and in all the settlements in the land. [14] I will tend them in a good pasture, and the mountain heights of Israel will be their grazing land. There they will lie down in good grazing land, and there they will feed in a rich pasture on the mountains of Israel. [15] I myself will tend my sheep and have them lie down, declares the Sovereign Lord. [16] I will search for the lost and bring back the strays. I will bind up the injured and strengthen the weak, but the sleek and the strong I will destroy. I will shepherd the flock with justice.*

God himself has to pastor them; he would never simply abandon them. In his example, we see what God expects of pastors today:

- Search for the sheep and look after them.

- Rescue them from the places where they were scattered and take care of them.
- Take them out of the world to pasture them in secure flocks.
- Pasture them in the best pastures where they will be well fed.
- Provide them with good places of rest.
- Bind up the injured.
- Strengthen the weak.
- Shepherd them with justice.

Interestingly, he is against the sleek and strong sheep; he will destroy them!

Judgment on the sheep

[17] "'As for you, my flock, this is what the Sovereign Lord says: I will judge between one sheep and another, and between rams and goats. [18] Is it not enough for you to feed on the good pasture? Must you also trample the rest of your pasture with your feet? Is it not enough for you to drink clear water? Must you also muddy the rest with your feet? [19] Must my flock feed on what you have trampled and drink what you have muddied with your feet?

[20] "'Therefore this is what the Sovereign Lord says to them: See, I myself will judge between the fat sheep and the lean sheep. [21] Because you shove with flank and shoulder, butting all the weak sheep with your horns until you have driven them away, [22] I will save my flock, and they will no longer be plundered. I will judge between one sheep and another. [23] I will place over them one shepherd, my servant David, and he will tend them; he will tend them and be their shepherd. [24] I the Lord will be their God, and my servant David will be prince among them. I the Lord have spoken.

The pastors are not the only ones in sin. God has a special place in his heart for the lean and weak sheep and is opposed to the fat, selfish sheep who deprive the weaker ones of good food and water.

His solution for these abuses is to pasture his sheep himself, through the Great Shepherd, who has David's heart and is his descendant, and the pastors whom Jesus delegates to care for his flock.

25 "'I will make a covenant of peace with them and rid the land of savage beasts so that they may live in the wilderness and sleep in the forests in safety. 26 I will make them and the places surrounding my hill a blessing. I will send down showers in season; there will be showers of blessing.27 The trees will yield their fruit and the ground will yield its crops; the people will be secure in their land. They will know that I am the Lord, when I break the bars of their yoke and rescue them from the hands of those who enslaved them. 28 They will no longer be plundered by the nations, nor will wild animals devour them. They will live in safety, and no one will make them afraid. 29 I will provide for them a land renowned for its crops, and they will no longer be victims of famine in the land or bear the scorn of the nations. 30 Then they will know that I, the Lord their God, am with them and that they, the Israelites, are my people, declares the Sovereign Lord. 31 You are my sheep, the sheep of my pasture, and I am your God, declares the Sovereign Lord.'"

God will do everything necessary to care for his sheep and give them the best. We cannot complete the Great Commission without the hard work of pastors. Apostles, prophets, and evangelists may get the attention, preaching to multitudes and operating in signs and wonders, but it is the pastors who keep churches healthy, feeding and caring for sheep who work with them in making disciples.

11

The Importance of Work

John 5:16–47

To complete the Great Commission we are going to have to work. Work hard—spiritually, emotionally, and even physically. God is preparing us to reign with Christ. Heaven (and God's kingdom) is not only about resting and endless worship services. God is a god who works.

This chapter finds us in Jerusalem for a festival, surrounded by all the religious leaders. The situation was volatile, and Jesus knew it. He had healed a man in the famous Bethesda pool, an ugly place crowded with desperately ill people. The man went straight to the temple to tell everyone about the miracle. He did not even know that it was Jesus who healed him, but when he found out, without thinking, he told them. Who could argue with such an impressive miracle? Well, Jesus did it on the Sabbath, which infuriated the Jewish leaders. When we serve the Lord, we will encounter opposition, even from religious leaders. As usual, Jesus did not submit to their pressure, and did nothing to placate them, defend himself, or apologize. He did not say: "Oh, forgive me. I didn't realize I was breaking the Sabbath. I won't do it again." No, Jesus made the situation worse with what he was about to say.

Jesus is still working

16 So, because Jesus was doing these things on the Sabbath, the Jewish leaders began to persecute him. 17 In his defense Jesus said to them, "My Father is always at his work to this very day, and I too am working."

The Father does not have a day of rest; Jesus said he is always working, every day. He did rest on the seventh day of creation, but he is continually working to save and heal, even on the Sabbath. There may be times when it seems that God is not working; we call out to him and he does not seem to do anything, but Jesus says he is always working.

Work is important. It is part of God's nature, and we are made in his image. It is good to work. Unemployment is tough; it destroys the self-image. God wants you to be productive, and he wants you in a worthwhile job. Every believer should be busy building God's kingdom. We have an important job to finish: Making disciples of all nations. Are you working toward that goal? Surely that is a priority for God, and he is working overtime on it. The premise of the excellent book Experiencing God is that you should look for where God is already working and join him in that work. Where can you see God working right now?

The Pharisees believed God was working in the temple, through well-educated people. They were very religious and very busy, but they missed God's blessing because of their rigid interpretation of the Bible. God was working in the streets, in the country, and ugly places like Bethesda. Today, many would say that God is working in the mega churches and through famous apostles and prophets. That may be, but how tragic to be wrong and ignore the people doing God's work in humble places.

Jesus equal to the Father

What Jesus said seems innocent enough, but it was too much for the Jewish leaders:

18 For this reason they tried all the more to kill him; not only was he breaking the Sabbath, but he was even calling God his own Father, making himself equal with God.

Again, Jesus did not defend himself. He did not say: "Oh, I'm sorry. I don't mean to say that I'm God. I am only the son of God, just like you are God's sons." No, he said he *is* God, and he so offended them that they were even more determined to kill him, because:

1. He broke their rules of Sabbath observance (although he broke none of God's laws).

2. Jesus called God his own Father—as his only begotten son, which is different than our relationship with God as Father—making himself equal with God. That was a big problem for the Jews, and for many today, who say the Bible never affirms that Jesus is God. But they are wrong: Jesus clearly claimed divinity. There are only three options: He has to be crazy, a liar, or truly God's Son. Do you have that assurance that Jesus is God? Can you defend his divinity to others?

Nothing of his own accord

¹⁹ Jesus gave them this answer: "Very truly I tell you, the Son can do nothing by himself; he can do only what he sees his Father doing, because whatever the Father does the Son also does.

Jesus' example provides us with something to avoid, and then gives us a way to guarantee productive work:

1. Jesus did nothing independently, by himself. Being God, he had the *potential* to do anything, but he did not have the *freedom* to do anything by himself. He is God's Son, but he could not do whatever he wanted to do; he only did what he saw his Father do. That implies a very intimate relationship—he was always observing his Father. If that was true for Christ (who never makes mistakes), how much more is it true for us (who are very error-prone). The Bible talks forcefully about the importance of doing God's will, and the danger of doing our own thing (see the warning in Matthew 7 on page 154 of this book). Since childhood, we have said: "I can;" now we have to say: "I can't." I can't invent new ways of doing God's work, or copy the world's methods. I can't do anything on my own.

2. Jesus wanted to imitate his Father; he did what he had seen him do. Whatever, everything, that the Father does, Jesus does also. But he did not automatically know what the Father's work was; he had to observe him. If the Father does it, he does it. In that way, he is assured of pleasing his Father and being fruitful.

What does that mean for us? Everything that Jesus did, we can do (confirmed by Scriptures like 1 Jn. 2:5–6 and Jn. 14:12). The most important source of information about what God does is the Bible. We have to study it and learn how God works, what he does, and what Jesus did.

Doesn't it make a lot of sense to work like that? Why would we want to do anything on our own accord? Do we really think we know more than God, or that we can do ministry better? Are we that proud? No, we need to examine what we do, to see if we are doing our own thing. Who are you to think that you are better than Jesus Christ?

20 For the Father loves the Son and shows him all he does. Yes, and he will show him even greater works than these, so that you will be amazed.

How beautiful to see the parallel between the relationship of God the Father and his son Jesus, and the father/son relationships in our lives! In a healthy family, a son observes everything his dad does and imitates it. Unfortunately, he will imitate the bad examples as well. A good father loves his son and wants to show him everything he does; he has nothing to hide. When my son was only five, he already had his "church" and would preach to his stuffed animals. Sometimes he would invite his mother and me to his church. Examine your actions to make sure you are not offering a bad example to your children.

God the Father also shows everything he does to his Son, Jesus. It is an expression of his love. The Father also loves you, his adopted child, and he wants to show you what he is doing. Open your eyes! Jesus promised that we would do greater things than he did, to amaze the world around us. If those Jews were scandalized and amazed by that healing, the Father has much more planned that will leave them even more scandalized and amazed!

God, the giver of life

²¹ For just as the Father raises the dead and gives them life, even so the Son gives life to whom he is pleased to give it.

Only God can give life. The fact that Jesus gives life to those he wants to is another confirmation of his divinity. We can be the vessel through which God brings life to others when we share his Word or introduce someone to Jesus. We always want to minister life, and never minister death.

To raise the dead and give life is an amazing expression of supernatural power, which was displayed when Jesus gave life back to a dead man, like Lazarus, and when the Father raised Jesus from the dead through the power of the Holy Spirit. Incredibly, he has given us that power as well (Matt. 10:8, Acts 9:40–41; 20:9–12). Do you have faith that God could use you to raise someone from the dead?

All judgment given to the Son

²² Moreover, the Father judges no one, but has entrusted all judgment to the Son, ²³ that all may honor the Son just as they honor the Father. Whoever does not honor the Son does not honor the Father, who sent him.

That comes as a surprise to many Christians: The Father does not judge anyone, but has delegated all judgment to Jesus. Sometimes we think of the Father as a stern judge and Jesus as our loving friend, but it is Jesus who will judge you. How comforting to know that your judge is also your savior!

Delegating is a way of honoring those under you. The Father delegated judging to his Son primarily so that everyone would honor Jesus just as they honor him. The pastor who delegates a task to an elder wants the church to honor that elder just as it honors the pastor. The Father does not take back the task of judging at will; he judges no one. When you delegate something, resist the temptation to get involved in it again, but be sure to provide a good example and instructions so they know what to do. Jesus learned how to judge by observing his Father (perhaps in Eden, or in the great flood).

Judging is a significant job and should never be done casually. A judge is worthy of great honor—thus we address judges "Your Honor." Honor is very important to God. Jesus is rebuking the Jewish leaders because they had the boldness to judge him for something good he had done, something that brought honor to God. We need to honor God and those he has placed in leadership.

How do we fail to honor Jesus?

- Doubting that he is God and was sent by the Father.
- Putting down his words and works.
- Not taking seriously who he is and what he commands.

In doing so, we dishonor the Father as well. How do we honor the Father and the Son?

- Believing their words and putting them into practice.
- Glorifying them by your example in the world and giving a good testimony of who they are.
- Giving all the glory to them and worshipping them in spirit and in truth, not only in church, but in all of daily life.
- Giving them first place in your life.
- Confessing your love for God and faith in him to others.

How to cross from death to life

24 "Very truly I tell you, whoever hears my word and believes him who sent me has eternal life and will not be judged but has crossed over from death to life.

Will you be judged? Have you crossed over from death to life? Do you have eternal life? What a great privilege to help someone cross from death to life, to be saved, and avoid eternal judgment. In your evangelism, do you share God's Word? Do you direct people to believe in the Father? Do you tell them about the life they will receive and the judgment they will avoid?

This is another way of explaining how to be saved, how to pass from death to life: Hear Jesus' word and believe the Father, with faith that everything the Bible says about God is true.

The dead will hear Jesus' voice

25 Very truly I tell you, a time is coming and has now come when the dead will hear the voice of the Son of God and those who hear will live.

This is a hard verse. Who are these dead? People in the grave who heard Jesus' voice while he was in the tomb? Or those physically alive but spiritually dead? Not everyone who heard Jesus' voice received eternal life. To live when we hear his voice and his Word, we must respond in faith and obedience.

26 For as the Father has life in himself, so he has granted the Son also to have life in himself. 27 And he has given him authority to judge because he is the Son of Man.

Nobody gave Jesus life; he was not born or created, but has life in himself. However, we do see order in the godhead, with Jesus submitting to his Father. The Father delegated all judging to Jesus and also gave him the authority to do it. When you delegate a task to someone, make sure you give them the corresponding authority.

28 "Do not be amazed at this, for a time is coming when all who are in their graves will hear his voice 29 and come out—those who have done what is good will rise to live, and those who have done what is evil will rise to be condemned.

At the end of the age, when Jesus returns, he will give a shout and all the dead will rise to be judged.

- Those who have done what is good will receive life (again, the importance of good works!).
- Those who have done what is evil will be judged. We all sin at times, but we repent and ask God's forgiveness. It is the person who *practices* sin who will be judged: *No one who is born of God practices sin, because His seed abides in him; and he cannot sin, because he is born of God* (1 Jn. 3:9).

Our good works do not save us, but we are judged by them. How will it go for you that day before God's throne? Will you receive life?

30 By myself I can do nothing; I judge only as I hear, and my judgment is just, for I seek not to please myself but him who sent me.

Just as Jesus taught only what the Father gave him, and did nothing on his own, so he judges only as he hears. He just said that the Father delegated all judgment to him, but he still relies on what he hears from his Father to make the judgments. What an incredible picture of submission, honor, and working together! This is his example of how to honor those who have entrusted ministry to us, and, especially, how to honor God.

This is how Jesus lived, and how you should live: To please the Father, to please Jesus, and not yourself. Christ's entire life was submitted to the Father. To please the Father and do his will, you have to know what it is. The Bible is the most important source, along with the Holy Spirit to guide you moment by moment. Would you say you know God's will in a general sense? Do you receive specific guidance for decisions you need to make? Or are you stumbling around in the darkness, doing what seems right to you? Our fallen nature is intent on pleasing itself. Whether at home, in our free time, or at church, we naturally tend to do what we want to do, instead of taking the time to listen for God's voice and study the Scriptures, and do what the Father tells us to do. When you are working to fulfill the Great Commission, God will guide you and prepare the way before you. Can you walk like Jesus walked and make pleasing God your primary goal in life?

The testimony about Jesus

[31] *"If I testify about myself, my testimony is not true.* [32] *There is another who testifies in my favor, and I know that his testimony about me is true.*

To further annoy the religious leaders, Jesus claims the testimony of a mysterious "other," leaving us to guess who that might be, and what kind of testimony it would be. If someone testifies in their own favor, it is not valid. However, his Father testified in his favor, with an audible voice at his baptism, in response to his prayers (like Lazarus' resurrection, Jn. 11:41–44), and in his miracles.

It is tempting to testify in your own favor: name dropping, mentioning the prizes you have received, and the studies you have completed. Be careful: that testimony is not valid, and be wary of others who testify in their own favor.

33 "You have sent to John and he has testified to the truth. 34 Not that I accept human testimony; but I mention it that you may be saved.35 John was a lamp that burned and gave light, and you chose for a time to enjoy his light.

Many respected John the Baptist. Even though Jesus generally did not accept men's testimony, he gratefully received John's.

36 "I have testimony weightier than that of John. For the works that the Father has given me to finish—the very works that I am doing—testify that the Father has sent me. 37 And the Father who sent me has himself testified concerning me.

Another important testimony is Jesus' works: the miracles, but most importantly, his death on the cross and resurrection.

Jesus condemns his accusers

Despite all this evidence, they did not honor him and refused to come to him (a decision of their will). Jesus was annoyed and changed his tone, condemning his accusers:

You have never heard his voice nor seen his form, 38 nor does his word dwell in you, for you do not believe the one he sent. 39 You study the Scriptures diligently because you think that in them you have eternal life. These are the very Scriptures that testify about me, 40 yet you refuse to come to me to have life.

- They have never heard his voice. Jesus is referring to the Father's voice, though the Father was speaking through him. They were listening to his voice at that very moment, but hearing spiritually involves more than listening to someone's voice, as Jesus said many times: "He who has ears to hear, let him hear."

- They have not seen his form. He is talking about the Father, but they do not have the spiritual eyes to truly see. Jesus said that those who have seen him have seen the Father (Jn. 14:9). God was standing there in front of them!

- His word does not live in them.

- They do not believe in the Father who sent Jesus— although they thought they were good, God-fearing Jews! Jesus said it is not possible to believe in God the Father if you do not believe in his Son.

- The Scriptures are important, but it is possible to diligently study them without the illumination of the Holy Spirit and miss the message. They ignored the clear testimony of the Old Testament about Jesus.

As if that were not strong enough, Jesus goes even deeper in his condemnation:

[41] *"I do not accept glory from human beings,* [42] *but I know you. I know that you do not have the love of God in your hearts.* [43] *I have come in my Father's name, and you do not accept me; but if someone else comes in his own name, you will accept him.* [44] *How can you believe since you accept glory from one another but do not seek the glory that comes from the only God?*

- They do not accept Jesus, who came in his Father's name.
- They give each other glory, but do not seek the glory that comes from God, which makes it impossible for them to have true faith.
- They looked religious, but did not have the love of God in their hearts.

We are very ready to accept glory from men: their praise, a position, or their proclamations of the great man of faith that you are. Seek the glory that comes from God, and do not fall into the trap of giving glory to each other. Nobody else may truly know you, but Jesus knows you and can see right through you. Do you have the love of God in your heart?

[45] *"But do not think I will accuse you before the Father. Your accuser is Moses, on whom your hopes are set.* [46] *If you believed Moses, you would believe me, for he wrote about me.* [47] *But since you do not believe what he wrote, how are you going to believe what I say?"*

Moses and his law were so important to them, but it is Moses who will accuse them.

What is God's work for you?

Are you living to please God? Do you honor him in all that you do? The Father has been working ever since creation, and continues working, with you or without you. Too often, there is something we want to do, and we ask God's blessing on it, but it may not be the work God has for us. What would be the best job for you? God has the best work, made to order for you, because he knows you perfectly. He invites you to work with him in his work. Where is he working around you and in your life right now? How can you join that work?

12

Four Vineyards

Matthew 20:1–16; 21:28–46

G od likes vineyards. The word appears 108 times in the New International Version. It would be interesting to study everything the Bible has to say about them. Here, in four parables, Jesus uses a vineyard to describe the kingdom of God. As we saw in the last chapter, work is important in the kingdom, and it is a theme that the four vineyards have in common. God is the owner, and we are the workers, laboring to complete the Great Commission and speed Christ's return.

Getting laborers for his vineyard

[1]"For the kingdom of heaven is like a landowner who went out early in the morning to hire workers for his vineyard.

Jesus said the harvest is plentiful, but the workers are few (Matt. 9:37). Here, God does not use full-time workers. The Lord of the universe has to get up early and go to the marketplace to find day laborers. Whether along a highway, at a gas station, or in a hardware store, many people today depend on someone like this landowner to make a living.

Wouldn't you think that God would have an abundance of laborers who want to work in his vineyard, excited about completing the Great Commission? Wouldn't God be the best boss anyone could have?

² He agreed to pay them a denarius for the day and sent them into his vineyard.

The first group is the only one that knew ahead of time what their pay would be. It appears to be the customary pay for a day's labor.

³ "About nine in the morning he went out and saw others standing in the marketplace doing nothing. ⁴ He told them, 'You also go and work in my vineyard, and I will pay you whatever is right.' ⁵ So they went.

"He went out again about noon and about three in the afternoon and did the same thing. ⁶ About five in the afternoon he went out and found still others standing around. He asked them, 'Why have you been standing here all day long doing nothing?'

⁷ "'Because no one has hired us,' they answered.

"He said to them, 'You also go and work in my vineyard.'

We do not know why he did not contract everyone he needed at the same time. Perhaps, being God, he was compassionate and wanted to help as many as possible. He may not like seeing able-bodied men idle, because "an idle mind is the devil's workshop." God designed us to work. His vineyard allowed him to offer work to many men, a good example for business owners today. The vineyard's almost limitless need for workers gives him many opportunities to test, train, and prepare us for a job in his kingdom.

Throughout the day, he went by the marketplace and always found others without work:

1. At nine, he contracted some to work for *"whatever is right."*
2. At noon, the same.
3. At three, the same.
4. Others waited all day, and at five, they were still idle. They were also sent to his vineyard.

Fair pay for a worker in the vineyard

[8] *"When evening came, the owner of the vineyard said to his foreman, 'Call the workers and pay them their wages, beginning with the last ones hired and going on to the first.'*

The owner had foremen whom he ordered to pay the workers, beginning with those hired last. They did exactly as he instructed them, and there was a surprise blessing for them:

[9] *"The workers who were hired about five in the afternoon came and each received a denarius.*

They had only worked an hour, but they received a day's pay! And so it was for the others hired during the day: they each received a day's pay.

[10] *So when those came who were hired first, they expected to receive more. But each one of them also received a denarius.*

The landowner did not follow any of our labor laws. Obviously, those who had worked all day expected more, especially since they had seen the owner's generosity. It would not be fair to work more and not receive more, but they were paid the same as everyone else. Strike! Protest! Knowing that, why work all day? Better to show up at the marketplace at five, work an hour, and get a day's pay.

[11] *When they received it, they began to grumble against the landowner.* [12] *'These who were hired last worked only one hour,' they said, 'and you have made them equal to us who have borne the burden of the work and the heat of the day.'*

Their complaint seems totally justified. It reminds me of the prodigal son's older brother (Lk. 15:28–30), who had always worked and done his best for his father, but never received anything special. His brother, who squandered his inheritance, came home to a grand celebration.

We expect to be paid for what we have done. What would you do? Why do you think the owner did not pay them more?

[13] *"But he answered one of them, 'I am not being unfair to you, friend. Didn't you agree to work for a denarius?* [14] *Take your pay and go. I want to give the one who was hired last the same as I gave you.* [15] *Don't I have the right to do what I want with my own money? Or are you envious because I am generous?'*

The owner was not unfair; they agreed to work for what he offered them. He is the owner. He is God. He is generous. Praise God for the blessing many received as a result of that generosity! It is his money, his kingdom, and his vineyard. He has every right to do whatever he wants. He does not force anyone to work in his kingdom, but when we answer his call and start to work, we have to submit to his standards.

Kingdom economy

[16] *"So the last will be first, and the first will be last."*

The kingdom economy does not make sense to worldly economists. As we saw in the second book in this series (Kingdom Culture), everything is reversed in the kingdom, and often it is not what we would think is fair.

Do you want to work for God? Do you understand what the compensation is? Are you ready to accept his priorities? How would you feel in these situations?

- Someone uneducated and recently released from prison comes to your church, having paid his debt for a horrible crime he committed, and is given a position, the same pay you receive, and the office you always wanted.
- You have studied, faithfully served God, and done everything right, but a new believer receives the promotion you feel you deserve.
- You have sacrificed to go to a difficult mission field, and no one recognizes your work, while a friend pastors a comfortable, wealthy church and is renowned as a successful pastor.

Be careful of envy. God may promote someone younger, with less experience. Comparing yourself with others is always dangerous. God has a call and compensation for each person. What is important is your relationship with him, understanding what he wants for you, and your faithful service. What happens with another brother is between him and his Lord; it has nothing to do with you. If you see someone receive a beautiful blessing from God's generous hand, praise the Lord! Rejoice in his blessing.

How can you apply God's generosity and fairness in your situation? Do you give preference to the "first"? Is it time to give more to the "last"? Do you consider yourself among the first, or the last? Could your church have a ministry like the landowner had here, and go out to the streets looking for idle people who want to work?

What is your motive for working? In this parable, the workers had no relationship with the owner; they just wanted to earn something to feed their families. If your motive in serving God is others' recognition, money, or some reward from God, you may be disappointed. But if you have a servant's mentality, love your master, and want to do your best for him because he has done so much for you, you can be very useful in God's hands.

Do you keep your word? Matthew 21:28–46

28 "What do you think? There was a man who had two sons. He went to the first and said, 'Son, go and work today in the vineyard.' 29 "'I will not,' he answered, but later he changed his mind and went. 30 "Then the father went to the other son and said the same thing. He answered, 'I will, sir,' but he did not go. 31 "Which of the two did what his father wanted?"

"The first," they answered.

The context of this parable is the temple—Jesus is speaking with the chief priests and elders, who want to know where he got the authority to do what he is doing. They were well aware that Jesus condemned their hypocrisy and appearance of religiosity.

I am sure we have all known someone like the sons in this parable:

- Your kids.
- A brother in your family.
- Church members who talk about all they will do, but do not keep their word.

The first one was honest: He did not want to work; he did not feel like it. He may be like many who struggle with rebellion, which makes it hard for them to submit, but they often have a good heart and end up repenting and obeying.

Sometimes we are quick to make commitments—like Peter when he said he would die with Christ. We want to look good, so we are afraid to tell someone in authority that we do not want to do something. In some cultures, it is very hard to say "no." They always want to look like good Christians, ready to serve, but it is often understood that they probably will not keep their word.

Many Christians know all the words to say to look good. In church, they go forward and say "amen" to the call to do something for the Lord, but they do not do it.

Jesus said to them, "Truly I tell you, the tax collectors and the prostitutes are entering the kingdom of God ahead of you. ³² For John came to you to show you the way of righteousness, and you did not believe him, but the tax collectors and the prostitutes did. And even after you saw this, you did not repent and believe him.

Jesus' audience was very confident of having a special place in the kingdom. They looked godly, but were very selective in their obedience. Once again, we often have things reversed. We look down on "sinners" and praise the religious people. These priests and elders never accepted John the Baptist, who was not one of them and violated their understanding of ministry. Today, it could be addicts, prisoners, and others with a bad reputation who have truly repented, who are entering the kingdom first.

If this parable was not enough to condemn those religious leaders, Jesus has another, even stronger parable.

Another vineyard, other workers and another trip leaving them in charge

³³ "Listen to another parable: There was a landowner who planted a vineyard. He put a wall around it, dug a winepress in it and built a watchtower. Then he rented the vineyard to some farmers and moved to another place. ³⁴ When the harvest time approached, he sent his servants to the tenants to collect his fruit. ³⁵ "The tenants seized his servants; they beat one, killed another, and stoned a third. *³⁶ Then he sent other servants to them, more than the first time, and the tenants treated them the same way.*

The servants the landowner sent were God's servants in the past, including the Old Testament prophets. The owner patiently gave these tenants the opportunity to work, but they did not honor the owner or his servants.

³⁷ Last of all, he sent his son to them. 'They will respect my son,' he said. ³⁸ "But when the tenants saw the son, they said to each other, 'This is the heir. Come, let's kill him and take his inheritance.' ³⁹ So they took him and threw him out of the vineyard and killed him.

Did the priests and elders know that Jesus was talking about himself? Possibly. If they did not honor the prophets, they will honor God's Son even less.

What angers God is the possibility that a pastor or apostle would be so proud that he believes the church is his. There is no room for Jesus; they do not want to submit to him or repent. They want to keep their religious empire and get rid of Christ.

⁴⁰ "Therefore, when the owner of the vineyard comes, what will he do to those tenants?"

⁴¹ "He will bring those wretches to a wretched end," they replied, "and he will rent the vineyard to other tenants, who will give him his share of the crop at harvest time."

Jesus impresses me with the way he let others condemn themselves, because these priests were prophesying exactly what happened: The Jews lost their kingdom and God gave it to the church.

⁴² Jesus said to them, "Have you never read in the Scriptures:

"'The stone the builders rejected
*   has become the cornerstone;*
the Lord has done this,
*   and it is marvelous in our eyes'?*

⁴³ *"Therefore I tell you that the kingdom of God will be taken away from you and given to a people who will produce its fruit. ⁴⁴ Anyone who falls on this stone will be broken to pieces; anyone on whom it falls will be crushed."*

Now Jesus clearly declares them guilty. God is looking for people who will produce kingdom fruit. If you do not think the same thing could happen to a church today, read the letters to the seven churches in Revelation chapters 2 and 3 again. For example, what Jesus said to the church at Ephesus:

Yet I hold this against you: You have forsaken the love you had at first. ⁵ Consider how far you have fallen! Repent and do the things you did at first. If you do not repent, I will come to you and remove your lampstand from its place (Rev. 2:4–5).

Jesus must be the cornerstone of any ministry. We have to give Christ his place in every kingdom work. God is no respecter of persons; if a church does not produce kingdom fruit, God will look for others who are serious about it.

⁴⁵ *When the chief priests and the Pharisees heard Jesus' parables, they knew he was talking about them. ⁴⁶ They looked for a way to arrest him, but they were afraid of the crowd because the people held that he was a prophet.*

Those who are involved in religion and build their own religious empires will strongly react to the message of the kingdom. That may include today's established church.

Do you need more time?

There is one more very short parable about the vineyard, with a message common to many of Jesus' teachings.

Then he told this parable: "A man had a fig tree growing in his vineyard, and he went to look for fruit on it but did not find any. So he said to the man who took care of the vineyard, 'For three years now I've been coming to look for fruit on this fig tree and haven't found any. Cut it down! Why should it use up the soil?'

"'Sir,' the man replied, 'leave it alone for one more year, and I'll dig around it and fertilize it. If it bears fruit next year, fine! If not, then cut it down.'" (Lk. 13:6–9)

God is very patient. He understands the time needed to grow and prepare to be fruitful in his kingdom, but the expectation is that every believer will produce fruit. If not, they are only taking up space in some church. Church leaders should seriously consider the possibility that God may cut down many unfruitful fig trees and burn them. Like this vine keeper, we can identify which ones they are and apply more fertilizer—something that will stimulate them to blossom and bear fruit. If we follow the Master's Plan and make disciples, it should be obvious who is unfruitful and why.

We have had 2000 years to complete the Great Commission. We have seen several times how hard it is for God to get good workers. The problem is not with the "sinners" or the harvest. The harvest is plentiful. The problem is with God's servants. Time just may be that short, that God has given us "one more year," and soon will cut down the unfruitful trees.

13

After the Fall

John 21

When Jesus rose from the dead, he first appeared to Mary Magdalene, but she did not recognize him—something changed in his post-resurrection appearance. Even his closest disciples did not recognize him, although they could touch him. He could appear and disappear and pass through walls, but he was not a ghost. He ate and drank, and still had wounds in his hands and side. He appeared to 500 people—never in the temple or the synagogue, but rather in a garden, on a road, in the Upper Room, and, now, for the third time to the disciples, on the beach.

¹Afterward Jesus appeared again to his disciples, by the Sea of Galilee. It happened this way: ² Simon Peter, Thomas (also known as Didymus), Nathanael from Cana in Galilee, the sons of Zebedee, and two other disciples were together.

Jesus had commanded them to go to Galilee (Matt. 28:10), and in obedience they went. We do not know how many days had passed, but Jesus did not come. You would think that after seeing the risen Lord, you would have faith for the rest of your life. How could you doubt? But it is so easy to forget the miracles and fall into disbelief, even for these disciples who had spent three years with Jesus. Christ was about to ascend to his Father and leave these disciples whom he had trained to establish the church. They would have the Great Commission to guide them. But first, with his pastor's heart, Jesus had to minister to their leader. Without Peter, the future of his entire mission would be doubtful.

Peter goes back to fishing

It happened one night, as seven of the disciples—including the three in Jesus' inner circle—were together, possibly in Simon's house. They were bored, tired of waiting for Jesus, and did not feel like doing anything. You may have spent a night like that with some friends: There's nothing on TV. You've checked Facebook, but there's nothing new. You've seen too many videos on YouTube. You don't feel like praying. It is an open door for the devil to tempt you. And it was Peter, the impulsive one, the leader, who finally had an idea:

³ "I'm going out to fish," Simon Peter told them.

It's not a sin to fish. In fact, fishing is a good hobby. However, several years before, when Jesus had called Peter, he told him that there would be a change in his fishing—from then on he would fish for men (Lk. 5:10). Peter left his nets and his boat to follow Jesus, but now we learn that he kept his nets, possibly in his house, and still had his boat. Why? He does not need them anymore. However, like many of us, he wanted to hold onto some of his old life, just in case.

Is there anything you have held onto? It may be something that bound you up in sin, something innocent, or just something in your mind, but it is dangerous. Christ calls us to leave everything to follow him. It is too easy to go back to your old nets and boat in a moment of discouragement and weakness.

Are you a leader or a follower?

It is even more dangerous if you are a person of influence: A pastor, parent, or, in this case, the disciples' leader. Your sin can cause others to stumble. I have known too many prisoners full of guilt because someone died or was imprisoned under their influence.

They said to him: We'll go with you.

You may be a follower. You are easily influenced. You do not have the strength to stand up and resist the other person. I have also known too many inmates who were innocent—in prison because they followed the wrong man.

So they went out and got into the boat, but that night they caught nothing.

That is strange: these are professional fishermen who knew that sea. There are nights when you do not catch much, but no fish at all? The truth is that what worked well for you in the past no longer works. You cannot go back to your old life. What brought you riches and pleasures in the past will be empty.

They finished the night worse than ever: Now they are tired, frustrated, and discouraged. Nothing is going right. When we do things your way, without Jesus, suddenly the car does not run, the computer crashes, and there are problems at home and on the job.

Do you have something to eat?

[4] *Early in the morning, Jesus stood on the shore, but the disciples did not realize that it was Jesus.*

It is great that Jesus shows up in our darkest hour, but they did not realize that it was Jesus. And why didn't he show up the night before, at the house, to spare them that wasted, exhausting, frustrating night? They could have had a beautiful time of communion with the Lord! Many times, we find it hard to understand the Lord's timing; it is easy to think that Jesus is late, but he is always right on time. Sometimes we have to go through those dark nights. God allows us to stumble, to reveal our unbelieving, rebellious heart. It can be a test of faith.

There may have been times when Jesus showed up in your life, but you did not know it was him. You may have been so angry or caught up in your sin that you were not thinking about the Lord. In this case, Jesus appeared at dawn. Many times, after a sleepless night, Jesus shows up at dawn. Do not miss out on that blessing; get up early to wait for the Lord.

⁵ He called out to them, "Friends, haven't you any fish?"

"No," they answered.

The Greek word translated "friends" here is an affectionate term used for your children. It should get the disciples' attention; it would be odd for a stranger to call them children. His question is like salt in a wound; he knows they have nothing to eat, that is why he has a delicious breakfast prepared for them. How humiliating to confess that they did not catch anything!

Another miraculous catch

⁶ He said, "Throw your net on the right side of the boat and you will find some." When they did, they were unable to haul the net in because of the large number of fish.

Is there a difference between the right and left sides of the boat? Of course not! And how could this stranger know there would be fish on the right? The directive could be offensive to these fishermen, but their response may reveal the humility that Christ had fostered in them.

When they throw the nets on the right, the transformation is radical: There are so many fish that they cannot haul the net in! Jesus wants to fill your net! But you have to fish his way, in obedience to his word, and not when and how you feel like it. They spent a whole night of hard work with nothing to show for it! And many of us work and spend a lot of energy and money, with no results. How easy it is when we do things in obedience to Jesus! It is much better to wait for his timing!

This is not the first miraculous catch (see Lk. 5:4). When we see something so out of the ordinary, it should get our attention, but only John had his spiritual eyes open:

⁷ Then the disciple whom Jesus loved said to Peter, "It is the Lord!"

John recognized Jesus, but did nothing! He just talked to Peter. Of course, it is good to share with others if you see the Lord, but when Jesus reveals himself to you, draw close to him, worship him, and listen to him!

As soon as Simon Peter heard him say, "It is the Lord," he wrapped his outer garment around him (for he had taken it off) and jumped into the water.

Simon was their leader. It was his idea to fish that night. He felt guilty because he had denied Jesus, and he did not recognize him that morning. But when he heard that it was the Lord, all he could think of was that he had to get to Jesus. Nothing else mattered.

Jesus wants to reveal himself to you

Have you fallen into sin? Are you far from Jesus? He wants to come to you right now. It is not by chance that you are reading this book. Perhaps you accepted the lie that it would be hard to get right with the Lord. Forget all that. Get into the water and go see Jesus, because he is waiting for you.

This is not the first time Peter went into the sea to go to Jesus. Months before, in the same sea, the disciples were alone in a boat, at night, in a storm, and Jesus approached them, walking on the water (Matt. 14: 22–33): *Peter said: Lord, if it is you, command that I go to you on the waters. And he said: Come.* When Peter got out of the boat, he walked on the water to go to Jesus. Everything was fine, but when he saw the strong wind, he was afraid and began to sink. Thank God, Jesus rescued him, and then rebuked him! *You of little faith! Why did you doubt?*

This time, Peter did not walk on water, but he still wanted to go to Jesus. It does not matter if you do not have the faith to walk on water, get into the sea.

⁸ The other disciples followed in the boat, towing the net full of fish, for they were not far from shore, about a hundred yards.

They were near the shore. Of the seven disciples, only Peter left the fish to go to Jesus. Not many love Jesus enough to leave such a valuable catch to be with him.

A delicious breakfast

⁹ When they landed, they saw a fire of burning coals there with fish on it, and some bread. ¹⁰ Jesus said to them, "Bring some of the fish you have just caught."

It was too late to prepare those fish for breakfast; Jesus already had fish on the coals, but we have to take what Christ miraculously gives us to the Lord. It is not to make us rich, but to use to serve him and bless others.

11 So Simon Peter climbed back into the boat and dragged the net ashore. It was full of large fish, 153, but even with so many the net was not torn.

Again, it is Peter who takes the initiative and obeys the Lord's command. Not only are there many fish, they are large, and there was probably another miracle: the net did not break. Notice John's precision in writing this gospel: someone counted the fish, and John records the number (153 fish).

If Jesus fills your net, bring it to him and lay it at his feet. He does not want to lose a single fish; each one is precious to him.

12 Jesus said to them, "Come and have breakfast." None of the disciples dared ask him, "Who are you?" They knew it was the Lord.

How strange, after three years together, and knowing it was Jesus, that nobody dared embrace him or say anything.

13 Jesus came, took the bread and gave it to them, and did the same with the fish.

Jesus did it for the crowds, multiplying bread and fish that those same disciples distributed to thousands of people. Just a few days before, Jesus gave them bread and wine, symbols of his broken body and shed blood. What a blessing to receive food from the Lord's hand!

14 This was now the third time Jesus appeared to his disciples after he was raised from the dead.

They may have eaten in silence. I am sure this was the best bread and fish they had ever eaten. Can you imagine that communion and delicious breakfast, early in the morning, at dawn, on the beach? Jesus delights in blessing us, and he loved preparing this meal. However, as on many other occasions, he had a hidden agenda.

Peter's restoration

Do you need Jesus to restore you? His Spirit can touch your hardened heart right now, to speak to you, challenge you, and restore you.

15 When they had finished eating, Jesus said to Simon Peter, "Simon son of John, do you love me more than these?"

"Yes, Lord," he said, "you know that I love you."

Jesus said, "Feed my lambs."

Finally, Jesus breaks the silence. We do not know if he took Peter aside or if he was with the other disciples, but Jesus has a question for him. He uses the Greek word *agape* to ask him if he really loves Jesus with an unconditional love, with God's love. And it is not only if Peter loves Jesus, but if he loves him more than the other disciples do. Why does Jesus ask that? Maybe because Peter said he would die for Jesus (Jn. 13:37). He was very self-confident. It is a risk of leadership, thinking you are superior to others.

Peter responded with the Greek word for love between brothers: *fileo*. Jesus says nothing about his lack of *agape* love; he accepts us wherever we are. Even with that love, Jesus can use Peter: He commands him to feed his lambs. Believers are Jesus' lambs, but the Lord has put shepherds in his flock to feed them. It is a sacred and heavy responsibility.

16 Again Jesus said, "Simon son of John, do you love me?"

He answered, "Yes, Lord, you know that I love you."

Jesus said, "Take care of my sheep."

This time Jesus does not ask if Peter loves him more than others; the truth may be that he doesn't. Again, Jesus uses the word *agape* for love, and Peter replies that he has a *fileo* love. And for the second time, Jesus tells him: if you really love me, you will take care of those who believe in me.

¹⁷ The third time he said to him, "Simon son of John, do you love me?"

Peter was hurt because Jesus asked him the third time, "Do you love me?" He said, "Lord, you know all things; you know that I love you."

Jesus said, "Feed my sheep.

Peter was not hurt so much that Jesus had to ask him three times, but because Jesus now changed from *agape* love to *fileo*. It is clear that Peter does not have an *agape* love for Jesus. It is good to recognize the limits of our love, but also painful. What about you? Do you love Jesus with an *agape* love? How do you know if you love him or not? It seems to be the faithfulness of your service to God's call on your life. For Peter, it was to feed the Lord's sheep; it could be evangelism or another ministry for you. Your service to those whom Jesus loves is proof of your love for him.

Follow me

¹⁸ Very truly I tell you, when you were younger you dressed yourself and went where you wanted; but when you are old you will stretch out your hands, and someone else will dress you and lead you where you do not want to go." ¹⁹ Jesus said this to indicate the kind of death by which Peter would glorify God.

Aside from the meaning of Jesus' words as explained in verse 19, there is also an important teaching here about youth and old age. The confident and independent young man does what he wants. He can take care of himself. With maturity, we are supposed to have more control, but when we give our lives to Jesus, we give up that control to him. We have to humble ourselves and submit to others. For many, it is part of God's work to break their pride.

Then he said to him, "Follow me!"

Why did he add "Follow me"? Peter was in turmoil, struggling with guilt and mixed emotions. He had just received a hard word. Fear would be a natural response: "I don't want to die like this! I don't want to lose control!" In the midst of all that, the only really important thing is to follow Jesus. Can you say that you are following Christ in your daily life? Are you putting his teachings into practice?

20 *Peter turned and saw that the disciple whom Jesus loved was following them. (This was the one who had leaned back against Jesus at the supper and had said, "Lord, who is going to betray you?")* **21** *When Peter saw him, he asked, "Lord, what about him?"*

Peter is not satisfied with simply following Jesus. Like many of us, he often compared himself to others. Facebook promotes this competition; we read our friends' stories, see their beautiful photos, and it is easy to envy them. Jesus has a very simple answer to that:

22 *Jesus answered, "If I want him to remain alive until I return, what is that to you? You must follow me."*

Don't stress over what is going on with your brother; God has different plans for each person. All we have to do is be faithful to Jesus and follow him. How are you doing with that?

23 Because of this, the rumor spread among the believers that this disciple would not die. But Jesus did not say that he would not die; he only said, "If I want him to remain alive until I return, what is that to you?"

24 This is the disciple who testifies to these things and who wrote them down. We know that his testimony is true.

25 Jesus did many other things as well. If every one of them were written down, I suppose that even the whole world would not have room for the books that would be written.

And so ends the Gospel of John. How wonderful that the beloved disciple, someone who was so close to Jesus, wrote this story!

What is God's Word for you in this chapter?

- Are you a follower, like the other disciples in the house that night? You have followed your parents, your spouse, or a friend from the church, and have participated in their activities. But have you accepted Jesus as your Lord and Savior? Perhaps you have looked with envy on a Peter getting off the boat to go to Jesus, because you do not know what it is like to have that kind of love for the Lord. Jesus is calling you to give him everything and follow him.

- Are you a leader, like Peter? Have you failed someone in your church or family? Have you been through a time of doubt and discouragement? It is a great responsibility to be a leader. It's time to get moving and help others. You may have to ask for someone's forgiveness.

- You may have failed Jesus; like Peter, you denied him. You may think it is too late; you can no longer be useful to the Lord. Just as Jesus arranged that time on the beach to talk to Peter, he has done it for you in this Scripture. He wants to restore you. It is not too late. It is time to return to your calling and be fruitful in your ministry.

- You may be tempted to go back to your nets and your boat, to your old life. Or you may already be in that boat and haven't caught anything. You are frustrated and angry. Nothing is going right. You cannot go back to your old life. Leave those things and return to the Lord.

- You may be working hard and are tired. You think you are working for the Lord, but you are doing it your way. You need to wait for a word from Jesus and do things his way. He wants to fill your nets. He has big fish, many fish, and wants to bless your net so it doesn't break, but you have to work according to his word.

- The Lord's question to you may be: "Do you love me?" Do you have an *agape* love for Jesus, or a *fileo* love? If you love Jesus, are you taking care of his sheep and serving faithfully in his calling for you?

- Are you worried about another brother's walk? Maybe in competition with him? Jesus says: "What is that to you?" His simple word is: "You follow me." It is time to return to the simplicity you knew at the beginning and walk close to Jesus. This may not be a time to lead, but to follow.

- You may be tired. You need spiritual food. Just as Jesus prepared that delicious breakfast for the disciples, he wants to feed you with his Word and refresh you with his

Spirit. Take some time to rest and have dinner or breakfast with Jesus. He wants to fill you and bless you.

These disciples had experienced the incomparable blessing of spending three years in intimate communion with Jesus. They had seen the risen Lord. But they could forget all that so quickly and go back to their old life. We have spoken in this book of the Great Commission that Christ has given us, and the possibility and the need to fulfill it. You might have become distracted by many things and want to return to the quiet life of fishing, to a normal life. You can't. Christ has spoken to you in this book and calls you to get up and work. He calls you to make disciples. He is waiting for you at the "beach" and wants to love you and restore you. Are you going to obey his command?

14

Three Alarming Warnings

Matthew 7:13–27

J esus' most extensive teaching on discipleship is found in the Sermon on the Mount, which includes the Beatitudes, the Lord's Prayer, and the Golden Rule. It starts with the basics: Blessed are the poor in spirit, blessed are those who mourn. But as he teaches, Jesus goes deeper, and the teaching becomes more challenging—it is obvious that the Christian life is not for the faint of heart or someone only seeking blessings. Jesus directs his closing words of the Sermon to leaders—even entering the kingdom is hard, and that is just an introduction to three alarming warnings.

13 "Enter through the narrow gate. For wide is the gate and broad is the road that leads to destruction, and many enter through it. 14 But small is the gate and narrow the road that leads to life, and only a few find it.

There are only two options in this life, two gates. The wide gate is very obvious. Most people, without even thinking about it, gravitate to it, unaware of another option. Beautiful women beckon you there, with flashing lights and signs promising you all the world's pleasures. Nobody tells you that the broad road leads to destruction.

There is nothing about the narrow gate to grab your attention. The people going in (and there aren't many) are taking almost nothing with them. They are humble and simply dressed.

Have you entered through the narrow gate? How do you enter?

Several things are involved in starting the walk of discipleship with Jesus:

- A radical surrender to his Lordship as your Master and King. He is in charge; he owns you.

- A genuine repentance, from a heart broken by the hurt you have caused God and others. That includes the recognition that you are a sinner; Christ and his power are your only hope. You may have tried many times to change in your own strength, be a better person, and give up your bad habits. Now you know you cannot do it, and you freely confess that. With God's help, you have decided to give up your excuses and stop sinning.

- Crucifying the flesh, putting the old man to death. The narrow gate opens onto a road that leads to the cross. You are born again when you go through that gate and emerge a new creation, a new man. Everything from the past has been buried—symbolically, in the waters of baptism—and you rise to a new life.

- You enter through a relationship with a person, Jesus Christ, who said: "*I am the gate*" (Jn. 10:9).

If you are a pastor and have preached about how easy it is to be saved and enter into that new life, you are deceiving your people, and possibly yourself. If you believe that once you go through the narrow gate you embark on an expressway to blessing and prosperity, you are in for a surprise. That road is narrow and *difficult* (NLT). Without the power of the Holy Spirit, it is almost impossible. Many who go through the narrow gate turn around and choose to return to the pleasures of the broad road.

Jesus also said, "*I am the way*" (Jn. 14:6). The road is not a highway, but a person. You walk that narrow path united to Christ. You are in God's will, but that does not guarantee the good life. There are three mortal dangers on the narrow road that trip up many people and send them back onto the broad road to destruction.

1: False prophets

15 "Watch out for false prophets. They come to you in sheep's clothing, but inwardly they are ferocious wolves. 16 By their fruit you will recognize them. Do people pick grapes from thornbushes, or figs from thistles? 17 Likewise, every good tree bears good fruit, but a bad tree bears bad fruit. 18 A good tree cannot bear bad fruit, and a bad tree cannot bear good fruit. 19 Every tree that does not bear good fruit is cut down and thrown into the fire. 20 Thus, by their fruit you will recognize them.

The risk

Throughout the Old Testament, false prophets abounded. Jesus warned us that in the latter days there would be even more (Matt. 24:11), and I believe the church is already full of them. It is every pastor's responsibility to identify them and protect his flock from them. That is why it is so important to be part of a healthy church, but Jesus also calls each one of us to be on the lookout. That is not easy. Satan has always been a master of disguises. These false prophets do not show up in church as wolves, but as innocent sheep. They speak the words you want to hear. It is very easy to be deceived, but Christ gives us an answer to this danger.

The remedy

Study their fruits. They can use all the right words and quote the Bible. The appearances are great, but look below the surface. Wake up. Jesus says that many of them are ferocious (vicious, devouring) wolves.

What are some of the fruits Christ expects of his servants?

- Transformed lives. Those who receive their words and are part of their ministry should demonstrate the character of Christ and walk in increasing holiness.
- The fruit of the Spirit (Gal. 5:22–23) should be evident in them and their followers.
- They should glorify Jesus and draw attention to him.
- Their family and personal life should reflect Jesus' love and presence.

It is very difficult to know the fruit of an internet or TV prophet, or of a prophet who visits your church—it is the pastor's responsibility to examine their fruit. These are some "fruits" that could signal problems and the need for caution on your part; fruits which may indicate that the prophet was not sent from God:

- Predictions of things that never happen.
- Emphasis on money, with many pleas for offerings; in the worst cases actually "selling" prophecies.
- A luxurious lifestyle.

- Words that sound good but do not line up with the Bible; few references to the Bible, or verses taken out of context.
- Family problems, including divorce and rebellious children.
- Churches divided and lives destroyed as a result of their "ministry."
- Attractive internet sites filled with messages supposedly received from God.
- TV programs and appearances on the programs of well-known ministers.
- Best-selling books or other resources.

Of course, we should be slow to condemn someone for one of these things—for example, a well-done internet site—and we should not be on a witch hunt, but godly fruit should be evident.

The necessity of a fruitful life

You could almost overlook Jesus' statement that every tree that does not bear good fruit is cut down and thrown into the fire. That not only applies to prophets; all of Jesus' disciples should be fruitful:

"I am the true vine, and my Father is the gardener. He cuts off every branch in me that bears no fruit, while every branch that does bear fruit he prunes so that it will be even more fruitful. You are already clean because of the word I have spoken to you. Remain in me, as I also remain in you. No branch can bear fruit by itself; it must remain in the vine. Neither can you bear fruit unless you remain in me. I am the vine; you are the branches. If you remain in me and I in you, you will bear much fruit; apart from me you can do nothing. If you do not remain in me, you are like a branch that is thrown away and withers; such branches are picked up, thrown into the fire and burned" (Jn. 15:1–6).

The Christian who does not bear good fruit is useless in God's kingdom. He is cut off and thrown into the fires of hell. What is your fruit like? What would others say about your influence in your home, work, or church? Are you abiding in Christ? Jesus promises that if we remain in him, we will bear much good fruit.

2: Deceived ministers

The second danger is truly alarming: the possibility of deceiving yourself, thinking that you are walking the narrow path and doing God's will. This person presents all the appearances of a good Christian and minister. There may be no obvious sin in his life; to most people, he may seem like a model Christian.

[21] *"Not everyone who says to me, 'Lord, Lord,' will enter the kingdom of heaven, but only the one who does the will of my Father who is in heaven.* [22] *Many will say to me on that day, 'Lord, Lord, did we not prophesy in your name and in your name drive out demons and in your name perform many miracles?'* [23] *Then I will tell them plainly, 'I never knew you. Away from me, you evildoers!'*

The risk

In each of these three potential dangers, appearances are deceptive. Don't trust your eyes! Without spiritual discernment, it is very easy to be deceived!

Everything here looks great:

- They call Jesus "Lord," and genuinely believe he is their lord. They may have been in church all their lives. Of course, confessing Jesus as Lord is very important, but it can be just words; the confession must be confirmed by action.

- They prophesy in Jesus' name. They probably believe that are speaking true prophetic words from the Lord.
- They cast out demons. They may have deliverance ministries, with people who have been set free.
- They perform miracles; in fact, *many* miracles! They may have TV shows, campaigns, and be known as miracle workers.

Jesus says that in the same way that many walk the broad road, *many* will fall into this deception. All their lives, they have done "the Lord's work;" now they come before God's throne confident of a great reward. They are totally in shock at Jesus' condemnation. This is not a matter of some sin that costs them a star in their crown or a higher place in heaven. Jesus says that he never knew them. All those years they were deceived, ministering in Jesus' name, thinking they were great servants of the Lord, but they never even knew Jesus. They never went through the narrow gate. They were always walking the broad road. Even worse, Jesus calls them "evildoers!" They are sent to hell!

How could they have been so deceived? What sin did they commit? They were doing their own thing. Their life was not submitted to Jesus. What they did (which in itself may have been good) was not what God wanted them to do. They were never taught that part of being saved is doing God's will. It is not a matter of words or doing good works to bless other people.

The remedy

The solution is very simple: Do God's will. Have a reverence and fear of God that results in doing things *his* way. Prophesying in Jesus' name, casting out demons, and doing miracles are sacred works. It is not a show or something to be taken lightly. Always examine yourself and wait on the Lord for a confirmation of something you want to do in his name. Being part of a good church and submitting your ministry to another servant of God are important safeguards.

Can you say with certainty that you are doing the Father's will? Is there something you need to submit to him? Or something you need to give up if you are not sure it is from him?

3: A house on the rock

This also can be very deceptive. Both men are in the church, hear the Word of God, and build houses. For a while (maybe a long while), both houses look great. The foolish man's house might even look more impressive than the wise man's.

[24] *"Therefore everyone who hears these words of mine and puts them into practice is like a wise man who built his house on the rock.* [25] *The rain came down, the streams rose, and the winds blew and beat against that house; yet it did not fall, because it had its foundation on the rock.* [26] *But everyone who hears these words of mine and does not put them into practice is like a foolish man who built his house on sand.* [27] *The rain came down, the streams rose, and the winds blew and beat against that house, and it fell with a great crash."*

The risk

It is dangerous to hear God's Word and not put it into practice. The foolish man never learned the importance of obedience and submission to God's will. He spent copious amounts of time and money building his house, but he followed his own plans, and ignored warnings about building on the sand. It may be easier to build on the sand than deal with the rock. A beach house is very attractive! And everything appears to be fine. Most of the church probably believes this man is a great Christian. However, in the storm, in the trial, he cannot deal with the pressure, and everything falls apart. It *collapsed with a mighty crash* (NLT).

The remedy

You are responsible for the teaching you receive. Some people spend all day listening to preachers on the Internet, radio, or television. They have much knowledge, but little obedience. Develop the habit of meditating and praying about what you hear from the Bible, and determine to put it into practice.

How is your house? Does it have a solid foundation? Others may have beautiful houses—but they are built on the sand. Don't envy them. It may be that right now you are building a firm foundation on the rock of the Word and Jesus Christ. It may not look like much to others, but in his time, God will build a beautiful house that will stand in adversity. Are the winds beating against your house right now? It could be God's mercy to expose the quality of your foundation and your obedience. He may be giving you the chance to repent and obey him before your life, your family, or your church comes crashing down.

28 When Jesus had finished saying these things, the crowds were amazed at his teaching, 29 because he taught as one who had authority, and not as their teachers of the law.

With good reason, they were amazed. There was a vast difference from the feel-good preaching or condemnation of the teachers of the law. This is the authority we need in the church today; someone who preaches not to entertain and make people feel better, but enters into the deep things of God.

Four steps to a fruitful life

The possibility of working and building a beautiful house (or life, family, or church), only to see it come crashing down, is very alarming. As is the possibility of prophesying, casting out demons, and doing miracles, and approaching God's judgment throne expecting a reward and the words "well done, good and faithful servant," only to hear Christ say he never knew you and be sent to hell. But there is no need for fear. Jesus gives us four simple steps to assure you of good fruit and a life pleasing to him:

1. Enter into God's family through the narrow gate. Decide to leave your old life behind, repent of all sin, and submit to Christ's lordship. He is the gate; live in union with him.
2. Walk the narrow road. Once you go through that gate, you will find this road is not easy. It is always possible to go back to the broad road; Jesus does not force you to stay on the narrow path. You can still see the lights and all the attractions of the broad road. There will be many trials and temptations. Fix your eyes on Jesus, find other believers who are committed to following him, and keep going forward.
3. Read, study, and listen to God's Word. Faith comes by hearing and hearing by the Word of God. With so many voices coming at us from the internet and TV, it can be hard to hear his voice. His Word is the light on your path.
4. Put the Word into practice. It is dangerous to hear the Word and not obey it. God will help you put it into practice.

Obedience is the key. If you are walking the walk, daily putting the Word you hear into practice, you will learn to discern and do God's will. Always examine yourself and wait on the Lord to be sure that what you are doing is the Father's will, and you are not doing your own thing.

Do these things, and you can rest in peace. You will have a fruitful life, impacting many, and bringing great glory to God.

15

The Danger of Hypocrisy

Matthew 23

This is a tough chapter. We want to walk like Jesus and form serious disciples. He said that we should not judge others; it is a sin to gossip or undermine others' ministries. But if we are going to walk like Jesus, there will be times when we need to expose false doctrine and hypocrisy. The Bible never teaches us to tolerate or ignore sin. Of course, this is Jesus talking here. He is God, he is perfect, and has every right to judge sin. Before we talk about others, let's take a good look at ourselves:

"Why do you look at the speck of sawdust in your brother's eye and pay no attention to the plank in your own eye? How can you say to your brother, 'Let me take the speck out of your eye,' when all the time there is a plank in your own eye? You hypocrite, first take the plank out of your own eye, and then you will see clearly to remove the speck from your brother's eye (Matt. 7:3–5).

And Paul says in Romans 2:1:

You, therefore, have no excuse, you who pass judgment on someone else, for at whatever point you judge another, you are condemning yourself, because you who pass judgment do the same things.

There is a delicate balance: on the one hand, to love and honor others and their ministries; on the other hand, the responsibility to protect our families and churches. We do not want to be negative and focus on others' sin; it is better to dedicate our efforts to proclaiming a word of faith and edification, and to exalt Jesus. But there are times when we have to say the truth. This chapter allows us to examine ourselves in the light of the Word, so that with a clear conscience, we can help others avoid these errors.

The woes in Luke

Jesus pronounced similar "woes" in Luke 11:37–54. A Pharisee invited him to dine at his house, but Jesus failed to wash his hands before eating, and the Pharisee was offended. In that passage, Jesus spoke first to the Pharisees, but experts in the law were also present, and they said: *"Teacher, when you say these things, you insult us also"* (11:45). So Jesus proceeded to renounce them too! Not surprisingly, after that, they were more opposed to Jesus. Luke (11:53–54) concludes: *When Jesus went outside, the Pharisees and the teachers of the law began to oppose him fiercely and to besiege him with questions, waiting to catch him in something he might say.*

Nobody likes to be exposed; talking about sin and hypocrisy is an easy way to make enemies, but that did not bother Jesus.

Practice what you preach

[1]Then Jesus said to the crowds and to his disciples: [2] "The teachers of the law and the Pharisees sit in Moses' seat. [3] So you must be

careful to do everything they tell you. But do not do what they do, for they do not practice what they preach.

God has established people in his church with the gift and calling of teaching the Word. It is a great responsibility before God. When I am preparing a message, my prayer is always: "Lord, keep me from error; help me correctly interpret your Word and never misguide one of your sheep." James 3:1 is a sobering word: *Not many of you should become teachers, my fellow believers, because you know that we who teach will be judged more strictly.* If God has given us the privilege of teaching, it is not to exalt ourselves, but to humble ourselves and share his Word with fear and reverence for God. If you are a teacher in the church, how will God judge you? It is very serious to take the position of a teacher. If you are a leader and you offer someone the opportunity to teach, be sure that God has called them.

Jesus tells us to honor the *position* of pastor or teacher in the church, despite their personal deficiencies. You should always listen to the pure Word of God and put its teachings into practice. The problem was the testimony and example of these teachers. They did not practice what they preached. Today, it is easy to deceive people. You can preach a powerful word on the internet, on TV, or in a mega church. Nobody knows if you are living what you are teaching. That is why it is important to know the fruit and testimony of your pastor and Bible teacher. And you? At home, on the job, and in church, do you practice what you preach?

Do not burden others with loads you do not carry

[4] *They tie up heavy, cumbersome loads and put them on other people's shoulders, but they themselves are not willing to lift a finger to move them.*

As a pastor or teacher, you may touch on weighty issues of the Word and ask the church to live out that Word, but do not burden others with things you are not doing or do not want to do. If we teach something, we should be ready to help people put it into practice and be honest about our struggles with it.

The danger of doing everything for appearances

[5] *"Everything they do is done for people to see: They make their phylacteries wide and the tassels on their garments long;* [6] *they love the place of honor at banquets and the most important seats in the synagogues;* [7] *they love to be greeted with respect in the marketplaces and to be called 'Rabbi' by others.*

What is your heart's motive? Of course, it is great to do good works, but is it to honor and glorify God, or to make you look spiritual? Is it a sin to sit in a special seat at a dinner if someone offers it to you? No, but again, it depends on where your heart is at. Does it puff up your pride and make you feel important? Do you get offended if you are not offered that special seat? Jesus taught us to take the lowest place and wait for others to offer us a better seat (Lk. 14:7–14).

Is it a sin to have a big Bible? Of course not, but if you secretly want to impress people with the great man of faith that you are because of those external things, there is a problem. Is your title very important to you? Do you get offended if someone does not greet you on the street as "pastor"?

Call no one "father"?

[8] *"But you are not to be called 'Rabbi,' for you have one Teacher, and you are all brothers.* [9] *And do not call anyone on earth 'father,' for you have one Father, and he is in heaven.* [10] *Nor are you to be called instructors, for you have one Instructor, the Messiah.*

These verses have caused considerable anxiety for leaders. Jesus seems to prohibit the use of any title. His point here is that we are all equal, and it is wrong to place some believers above others. It is hard to reconcile what Jesus says with some who insist on being called pastor, apostle, prophet, or teacher. In the Catholic church, priests are generally called "father." Is that a sin? Is it a sin to call my dad "father"? I do not think we need to be that rigid, but rather focus on the spirit of what Jesus says here: The only true teacher we have is Christ, and the only perfect Father is in heaven.

Who is most important?

11 The greatest among you will be your servant. 12 For those who exalt themselves will be humbled, and those who humble themselves will be exalted.

It is always tempting to pursue fame and position. You want to be a good Christian, a good pastor, and a successful Bible teacher, and that is fine. But the natural human tendency is to get prideful: "I am the pastor. I have worked hard and have a great church. They should recognize that and serve me." But why are you ministering? Do you want to please God? Or have others praise you? We must seek every opportunity to serve others and humble ourselves. Trust in God to humble you and lift you up in his time and his way.

Are you doing things to lift yourself up? What more can you do to humble yourself? How has God humbled you in the past when you lifted yourself up?

Keeping others from the kingdom

13 "Woe to you, teachers of the law and Pharisees, you hypocrites! You shut the door of the kingdom of heaven in people's faces. You yourselves do not enter, nor will you let those enter who are trying to.

Jesus makes it clear: These hypocrites will not enter the kingdom of heaven. It is sad, but that is the decision they have made. What troubles Jesus is that they discourage those who sincerely want to enter, those who are walking the narrow path. They do not go through the narrow gate, and stand in the door and close it so that no one else can enter.

In Luke, Jesus says they have *taken away the key to knowledge* (11:52). Apparently, they deliberately taught some things, perhaps with their own interpretation and for their own benefit, and ignored the most important things in the Word.

Taking advantage of the vulnerable

14Woe to you, scribes and Pharisees, hypocrites! For you devour widows' houses and for the sake of appearance you make long prayers; therefore you will receive the greater condemnation.

The widow and the orphan are close to Jesus' heart. They are vulnerable, and instead of caring for them and providing for them, the scribes and Pharisees devoured them. They looked so spiritual, with their long prayers, but that was just a pretext for taking advantage of them. The Amplified Bible says: *For you swallow up widows' houses and for a pretense to cover it up make long prayers; therefore you will receive the greater condemnation and the heavier sentence.*

It reminds me of poor widows who see the TV evangelist asking for money, and from a sincere heart, send the little they have. They do not know that the ministry is buying a plane or a luxury car with that money.

Distorted evangelism

15 "Woe to you, teachers of the law and Pharisees, you hypocrites! You travel over land and sea to win a single convert, and when you have succeeded, you make them twice as much a child of hell as you are.

They evangelize, but not to bring the person into a living relationship with God. Instead of instructing them in God's Word, they lead them into legalism and hypocrisy. It is great to bring someone to Jesus' feet, and it is important to disciple that person, but be careful of the example you offer. You do not want him to follow in your sinful footsteps. That can happen today when someone follows an apostle, pastor, or doctrine more than they follow Christ.

Oaths

16 "Woe to you, blind guides! You say, 'If anyone swears by the temple, it means nothing; but anyone who swears by the gold of the temple is bound by that oath.' 17 You blind fools! Which is greater: the gold, or the temple that makes the gold sacred? 18 You also say, 'If anyone swears by the altar, it means nothing; but anyone who swears by the gift on the altar is bound by that oath.' 19 You blind men! Which is greater: the gift, or the altar that makes the gift sacred? 20 Therefore, anyone who swears by the altar swears by it and by everything on it. 21 And anyone who swears by the temple swears by it and by the one who dwells in it. 22 And anyone who swears by heaven swears by God's throne and by the one who sits on it.

This is the longest "woe". How tragic to be a "blind guide"! It is not the first time Jesus calls them blind guides. He was talking about what makes a person unclean, which is not external but internal. The disciples said to him: *"Do you know that the*

Pharisees were offended when they heard this?" And Jesus responded: *"Every plant which my heavenly Father has not planted will be torn up by the roots. Let them alone and disregard them; they are blind guides and teachers. And if a blind man leads a blind man, both will fall into a ditch"* (Matt. 15:12–14).

Interestingly, Jesus said to leave them alone. We need to be very careful with the guide we choose. And you, are you a blind guide? Or are you following someone who is blind? What is certain is that both will fall. When Jesus spoke of blind guides on another occasion (Lk. 6:39–40), he added: *"A blind man cannot guide a blind man, can he? Will they not both fall into a pit? A pupil is not above his teacher; but everyone, after he has been fully trained, will be like his teacher."* If you are guided by someone who is spiritually blind, you will only reach their level. Jesus calls them fools!

First of all, Jesus said you should not swear:

"Again, you have heard that it was said to the people long ago, 'Do not break your oath, but fulfill to the Lord the vows you have made.' But I tell you, do not swear an oath at all: either by heaven, for it is God's throne; or by the earth, for it is his footstool; or by Jerusalem, for it is the city of the Great King. And do not swear by your head, for you cannot make even one hair white or black. All you need to say is simply 'Yes' or 'No'; anything beyond this comes from the evil one" (Matt. 5:33–37).

They were already in error because oaths were very important to them. The specific problem here is that they gave more importance to the gold in the temple offerings than to the worship of God.

The danger of ignoring what is most important

²³ *"Woe to you, teachers of the law and Pharisees, you hypocrites! You give a tenth of your spices—mint, dill and cumin. But you have neglected the more important matters of the law—justice, mercy and faithfulness. You should have practiced the latter, without neglecting the former.* ²⁴ *You blind guides! You strain out a gnat but swallow a camel.*

The scribes and Pharisees were very faithful with their tithes. Exactly 10%. That is fine, but they were proud of their obedience to those details. How easy it is to feel good because you fulfill some legalistic requirements! And how hard it is to obey the more important things of God's Word! Like love, and, in this case, justice, mercy, and faithfulness. In Luke (11:42), Jesus said they *neglect justice and the love of God*. Those are things of the heart that involve our relationships with others and with God. How sad that many "good Christians" lack mercy for their families or people less fortunate.

The NLT explains verse 24: *You strain your water so you won't accidentally swallow a gnat, but you swallow a camel!* It is easy to strictly obey the small details and ignore the important parts of the big picture.

It is common for some churches to emphasize the tithe. Actually, the tithe was a requirement of Old Testament law. *Everything* belongs to Jesus; it is easy to feel we can selfishly use the 90%, when we should give everything we have to Christ. If we talk a lot about the tithe, we should talk even more about the most important things in the law.

Cleanse the inside first

²⁵ *"Woe to you, teachers of the law and Pharisees, you hypocrites! You clean the outside of the cup and dish, but inside they are full*

of greed and self-indulgence. ²⁶ Blind Pharisee! First clean the inside of the cup and dish, and then the outside also will be clean.

You can be well-dressed and well-groomed, carry a big Bible, know all the worship songs, and pray impressive prayers, but how is your heart? Too often, behind all the religious veneer, the heart is wicked. The Pharisees condemned Jesus because he did not observe the custom of washing hands and plates. It is the same old question of appearances, and our tendency to judge others by them. Even the prophet Samuel fell into this error, and God had to rebuke him: *"The Lord doesn't see things the way you see them. People judge by outward appearance, but the Lord looks at the heart"* (1 Sam. 16:7, NLT).

Jesus spoke about the importance of inner holiness on several occasions:

"Don't you see that whatever enters the mouth goes into the stomach and then out of the body? But the things that come out of a person's mouth come from the heart, and these defile them. For out of the heart come evil thoughts—murder, adultery, sexual immorality, theft, false testimony, slander. These are what defile a person; but eating with unwashed hands does not defile them" (Matt. 15:17–20).

Luke (11:39–41, NLT) gives us another perspective:

"You Pharisees are so careful to clean the outside of the cup and the dish, but inside you are filthy—full of greed and wickedness! Fools! Didn't God make the inside as well as the outside? So clean the inside by giving gifts to the poor, and you will be clean all over."

Jesus could clearly see inside them, and it was not pretty. They were full of greed and wickedness. How do you clean the inside? Jesus says it is by giving gifts to the poor!

The Message paraphrases it: *Turn both your pockets and your hearts inside out and give generously to the poor; then your lives will be clean, not just your dishes and your hands.*

When is the last time you heard a sermon on that?

[27] *"Woe to you, teachers of the law and Pharisees, you hypocrites! You are like whitewashed tombs, which look beautiful on the outside but on the inside are full of the bones of the dead and everything unclean.* [28] *In the same way, on the outside you appear to people as righteous but on the inside you are full of hypocrisy and wickedness.*

Do you know any "whitewashed tombs"? Most people only look at the appearances and see impressive righteousness, unaware that they are full of dead men's bones, hypocrisy, and wickedness.

In Luke (11:44, NLT), Jesus uses another image with the same meaning: *"For you are like hidden graves in a field. People walk over them without knowing the corruption they are stepping on."*

Snakes! Brood of vipers!

[29] *"Woe to you, teachers of the law and Pharisees, you hypocrites! You build tombs for the prophets and decorate the graves of the righteous.* [30] *And you say, 'If we had lived in the days of our ancestors, we would not have taken part with them in shedding the blood of the prophets.'* [31] *So you testify against yourselves that you are the descendants of those who murdered the prophets.* [32] *Go ahead, then, and complete what your ancestors started!* [33] *"You snakes! You brood of vipers! How will you escape being condemned to hell?*

The scribes and Pharisees believed they were much better than their ancestors, who killed the prophets. They even built them tombs and decorated their graves! However, once again, it was all about appearances. Jesus says that they have the same spirit as their ancestors and, in fact, are going to kill God's Son. He has some of his strongest words for them: they are snakes and vipers! Definitely bound for hell.

[34] Therefore I am sending you prophets and sages and teachers. Some of them you will kill and crucify; others you will flog in your synagogues and pursue from town to town. [35] And so upon you will come all the righteous blood that has been shed on earth, from the blood of righteous Abel to the blood of Zechariah son of Berekiah, whom you murdered between the temple and the altar. [36] Truly I tell you, all this will come on this generation.

God is patient and may wait many years to deliver a deserved judgment, but at some point, the breaking point is reached, and one group may bear the brunt of God's wrath. The Jews' rejection of Jesus and persecution of his servants had brought them to that point. Many believe that the destruction of the temple in AD 70 was the fulfillment of this prophecy.

[37] "Jerusalem, Jerusalem, you who kill the prophets and stone those sent to you, how often I have longed to gather your children together, as a hen gathers her chicks under her wings, and you were not willing. [38] Look, your house is left to you desolate. [39] For I tell you, you will not see me again until you say, 'Blessed is he who comes in the name of the Lord.'"

These are the words of a rejected lover. Jesus had so much love and so many blessings for them, but they did not want him! They were very presumptuous and believed they were honoring God's Word and doing the right thing. They were very religious, but they failed in the most important things, especially by rejecting God's Son! Do not think that we cannot fall into the same presumption. We should honestly examine ourselves and repent of the errors Jesus condemned here. We do not want to be like these hypocrites and make disciples destined for hell. First, we have to avoid the same errors ourselves, and then form disciples who hate hypocrisy, disciples focused on fulfilling the Great Commission.

16

Back Home

Luke 4:14–30

The Scriptures are clear about the importance of work in the kingdom of God. Are you ready to do your part in fulfilling the Great Commission? If you still do not have your first disciple, that is a good place to start. Isn't it amazing that Almighty God would use us for such an important task? Introducing someone to Christ and discipling him are among the greatest blessings and privileges of being a Christian. But we are still in this world, with jobs and families and the responsibilities that come with them. We are subject to sickness and aging—if Christ does not come first, we will all die. So we end this book walking with Jesus early in his ministry to his hometown, and at the end of his life on the agonizing road to the cross.

Overnight fame

14 Jesus returned to Galilee in the power of the Spirit, and news about him spread through the whole countryside. 15 He was teaching in their synagogues, and everyone praised him.

Jesus was a sensation; news about him quickly spread through the region, and everyone praised him. This was shortly after his

175

baptism and the desert temptations. It is unclear how long it was before he returned to Galilee—some scholars believe this was a year later—or if he had spent time ministering in Judea. He returned in the power of the Spirit that he received at his baptism, and started his ministry in the synagogues. It made sense to go to the fellowship of believers; they already knew the Word and should be more open to his teaching. Later, when there was more opposition, we rarely find Jesus there. Paul followed Jesus' example, always starting in the synagogue.

Not only was Jesus teaching with authority, he was already doing miracles in Capernaum. He knew the news would reach Nazareth, but wisely waited to return home, probably sensing the kind of reception he might have.

16 He went to Nazareth, where he had been brought up, and on the Sabbath day he went into the synagogue, as was his custom.

We know very little about Jesus' daily life prior to his baptism, but, unsurprisingly, on the Sabbath he always went to the synagogue—this Sabbath he was probably seated on the benches, along with the other worshippers and his family. As a courtesy to this son who had returned home, he was granted the honor of reading from the Bible.

A prophecy from Isaiah 61 fulfilled

He stood up to read, 17 and the scroll of the prophet Isaiah was handed to him. Unrolling it, he found the place where it is written:

> *18 "The Spirit of the Lord is on me,*
> *because he has anointed me*
> *to proclaim good news to the poor.*
> *He has sent me to proclaim freedom for the prisoners*
> *and recovery of sight for the blind,*

to set the oppressed free,
 19   to proclaim the year of the Lord's favor."

20 Then he rolled up the scroll, gave it back to the attendant and sat down. The eyes of everyone in the synagogue were fastened on him. 21 He began by saying to them, "Today this scripture is fulfilled in your hearing."

His message was short! Sometimes that is better! Jesus applied these few verses (from Isaiah 61:1–2) to himself; the Holy Spirit was upon him and had anointed him to:

- Announce good news to the poor (the humble, poor in spirit, or poor economically).
- Proclaim freedom to the captives (those bound in sin or by a demon, or imprisoned).
- Give sight to the blind (miraculously restoring their vision, or opening the eyes of the spiritually blind).
- Free the oppressed (possibly oppressed by the Roman Empire in this case, by the circumstances of life, or by the devil).
- Proclaim the year of the Lord's favor (God loves them and has good news for them! They are living at a very special time!).

His ministry would focus on suffering, hopeless, needy people, not on the rich and comfortable who are unaware of any need in their lives. This was not the kind of message religious people in the synagogue usually heard; its main appeal would be to unchurched people on the street. Jesus hoped that his hometown synagogue would understand and support him, but, sadly, religious people sometimes want nothing to do with these outcasts.

There are various callings, and God sends some Christians to wealthy, religious people. Just as Jesus first went to the synagogue, we need the support of the church, and usually start our ministry there, but some will follow Jesus' footsteps. Your greatest acceptance may not be in church, but with people despised by the world. Many are suffering and need to hear that this is a year of God's favor. God is for you, not against you.

22 All spoke well of him and were amazed at the gracious words that came from his lips. "Isn't this Joseph's son?" they asked.

They were surprised that "Joseph's son," the carpenter, could speak so eloquently. Although many recognize a good preacher and enjoy an encouraging message, even lauding their "gracious words," when it exposes their sin and need, that approval may evaporate.

23 Jesus said to them, "Surely you will quote this proverb to me: 'Physician, heal yourself!' And you will tell me, 'Do here in your hometown what we have heard that you did in Capernaum.'" 24 "Truly I tell you," he continued, "no prophet is accepted in his hometown.

They did not accept who he was or what he said. They wanted to see him perform and do miracles like he had done in Capernaum, but Jesus felt no obligation to please them. Instead, he spoke the truth: The most challenging place for a pastor or prophet (or anyone!) to minister is his hometown. Of course, that person knows the language and culture, giving him some advantages, and it is usually much less costly. That is the obvious appeal of indigenous missions, but sometimes it is better to send a traditional cross-cultural missionary.

As you make disciples, help them with the challenge of maintaining their testimony in their home and family. Going home is not necessarily easy; it may be better to begin your ministry elsewhere. To walk like Jesus means holding onto the message and anointing you receive, resisting the pressure to go back and be the "carpenter" and "the son of Joseph."

25 I assure you that there were many widows in Israel in Elijah's time, when the sky was shut for three and a half years and there was a severe famine throughout the land. 26 Yet Elijah was not sent to any of them, but to a widow in Zarephath in the region of Sidon. 27 And there were many in Israel with leprosy in the time of Elisha the prophet, yet not one of them was cleansed—only Naaman the Syrian."

Why did Jesus infuriate them on purpose? Surely He knew their prejudices against the Gentiles. This was not the way to win people over in your first sermon, but popularity never mattered to Jesus.

28 All the people in the synagogue were furious when they heard this. 29 They got up, drove him out of the town, and took him to the brow of the hill on which the town was built, in order to throw him off the cliff. 30 But he walked right through the crowd and went on his way.

People, by nature, are fickle. If you always want to be popular, you will compromise the message and lose the anointing. If you preach to be praised by the congregation and do not confront them with their sin and prejudices, you will lose God's blessing on your ministry. If you rely on public opinion, be careful: from one Sunday to the next, you may go from being the beloved pastor to being a false prophet. That happened with many pastors who received the baptism of the Holy Spirit and began preaching Pentecost.

Here, the devil himself seemed to enter them, and everyone (not just the leaders or a small group) was so furious that they tried to kill Jesus, but he miraculously passed through their midst and left town. It does not say so, but I imagine it was a long time before he returned to Nazareth. It is hard, but sometimes we may never be fully accepted by our families, people who have known us since childhood, or the church where we met Christ.

Another visit to Nazareth in Matthew 13

Surprisingly, that was not the last time Jesus ministered in the synagogue at Nazareth. Chronologically, it is challenging to place what happens in Matthew 13:53–58, but it appears to be a good while after that first visit recorded in Luke.

53 When Jesus had finished these parables, he moved on from there. 54 Coming to his hometown, he began teaching the people in their synagogue.

Jesus returned to the synagogue to teach, but not much had changed; they still could not accept his special anointing.

They were amazed: "Where did this man get this wisdom and these miraculous powers?" they asked. 55 "Isn't this the carpenter's son? Isn't his mother's name Mary, and aren't his brothers James, Joseph, Simon and Judas? 56 Aren't all his sisters with us? Where then did this man get all these things?" 57 And they took offense at him.

Here it is even clearer: Jesus' neighbors in Nazareth did not expect him to be a great spiritual leader. They said: "Where did he get such wisdom?" He did not have the reputation of speaking with great wisdom; apparently, they had never heard him teach before. His neighbors asked: "Where did he get such miraculous powers?" They were amazed that he could speak well and do miracles! There are extra-biblical stories of Jesus healing little animals and doing other miracles as a child, but scholars agree that they are not authentic. In Nazareth, Jesus was just the eldest of several brothers. Four of Mary and Joseph's children are named here: James was a leader of the early church in Jerusalem and wrote the book of James, Judas (Jude) wrote the last epistle of the New Testament, but we know nothing else about Joseph and Simon.

But Jesus said to them, "A prophet is not without honor except in his own town and in his own home."

Jesus repeats what Luke recorded, adding *"in his own home."* We all hope for approval in our hometown and family; surely their rejection grieved Jesus.

All four gospels include a reference to a prophet not being honored in his own land:

John 4:44: *Jesus himself had pointed out that a prophet has no honor in his own country.*

Mark 6:4–6: *Jesus said to them, "A prophet is not without honor except in his own town, among his relatives and in his own home." He could not do any miracles there, except lay his hands on a few sick people and heal them. He was amazed at their lack of faith.*

Can unbelief strip the Son of God of power to work miracles? Of course, God is all-powerful, but many Scriptures teach that God responds to our faith, which is often necessary to receive a miracle.

[58] *And he did not do many miracles there because of their lack of faith.*

Many pastors have ministered in another country with impressive signs and wonders, but return home and seem to lose the anointing. Even Jesus could not do many miracles in Nazareth because of their lack of faith. Where there is much faith and expectation, there will be many miracles. If you do not expect any miracles or do not believe in them, there probably will be none. When Jesus sent the Twelve and the Seventy out, he told them to shake the dust off their feet and leave the place if they were not received.

We have to prepare our disciples to face this reality. If it was true for Jesus, it will surely be true for us. You may have to go where there is more faith and expectation of receiving from God.

His family thinks he has gone crazy: Mark 3

Though his neighbors' reaction may be understandable, Mary had an angel announce Jesus' birth and spent some 30 years with him at home. Surely they talked about his mission, and she must have observed something very special in this son she gave birth to while still a virgin. Nevertheless, his family did not honor him either.

Jesus was attracting crowds and was so busy in the ministry that he had no time to eat. That was too much for a Jewish mother:

21 When his family heard about this, they went to take charge of him, for they said, "He is out of his mind."

This was a family mission; they had to rescue Jesus.

31 Then Jesus' mother and brothers arrived. Standing outside, they sent someone in to call him. 32 A crowd was sitting around him, and they told him, "Your mother and brothers are outside looking for you."

Mary and Jesus' brothers stayed outside; they got the crowd's attention, but did not even try to go into the house. Everyone expected that Jesus would stop ministering to receive his family, but again, they were wrong:

33 "Who are my mother and my brothers?" he asked.

34 Then he looked at those seated in a circle around him and said, "Here are my mother and my brothers! 35 Whoever does God's will is my brother and sister and mother."

When we go all out for the Lord's work, even our commitment to family changes. Jesus will not allow them to distract him from the important task of announcing the kingdom. When we accept Jesus, we have a new family. Of course, we maintain the relationship with our birth family; on the cross, Jesus entrusted his mother to the apostle John (Jn. 19:25–27), but now our true relatives are those who do God's will.

Does your family understand your commitment to serving God? Are they worried that you have become a fanatic? Do they try to persuade you to do less for the kingdom? They may be very sincere in their concerns—and possibly correct. Surely there is a healthy balance; do you dedicate enough time to your family? How is your relationship with others who obey God?

Even your best disciple can be the devil's instrument: Matthew 16

Jesus had just announced his upcoming death, and Peter had an extreme reaction:

22 Peter took him aside and began to rebuke him. "Never, Lord!" he said. "This shall never happen to you!"

23 Jesus turned and said to Peter, "Get behind me, Satan! You are a stumbling block to me; you do not have in mind the concerns of God, but merely human concerns."

When God calls us to follow the Master's plan or do something that demands great faith, even someone we have discipled can be used by Satan to try to stop it. It is more potent because it comes from a person you love and know very well, but walking as Jesus walked calls for a strong response:

- Immediately silence them. Jesus did not even want to hear Peter's advice or give any room for following his plan.
- Recognize the source of the temptation. Jesus rebukes the devil, not Peter. At that moment, we need to renounce Satan.
- Watch for the things (sometimes from the people closest to you) that could make you stumble. Although Peter spoke out of love and loyalty, Jesus knew that it would be a serious stumbling block.
- Is the person thinking about things from God's perspective, or a human point of view? Does it go against the Bible? Is it selfish, promoting an easier way? Does it result in glory and honor for God and the expansion of his kingdom?

Work until you fulfill your purpose: Luke 13:31–32

At that time some Pharisees said to him, "Get away from here if you want to live! Herod Antipas wants to kill you!"

Jesus replied, "Go tell that fox that I will keep on casting out demons and healing people today and tomorrow; and the third day I will accomplish my purpose (NLT).

It almost echoed Peter's words, but this was from the Pharisees. They sowed fear and focus on self; here, it was a warning to save his life. They would stop God's work and divert Jesus from his purpose, just as his family and Peter would have done. When you are in God's will and have a clear goal, call, mission, and purpose for your life, do not allow anything or anyone to distract you.

How great to die knowing that you have fulfilled your purpose and done your part to make disciples and obey the Great Commission. Do you know what your purpose is? Are you still doing God's will despite the danger and opposition? Where does your strongest opposition come from?

17

Preparing for Death

To walk as Jesus walked. It is great to talk about the miracles, the training of the Twelve, and Jesus' undying love. But his whole life, every step he took, was moving towards a single goal: To die on the cross as a perfect sacrifice for our sins.

Death is ugly. It was never part of God's plan. It was the devil who came to kill. Death entered our race when Adam and Eve sinned in rebellion against God's command. Death is the last enemy (1 Cor. 15:26), but it is a road every one of us must walk (unless Jesus comes back first). We do not like to think about death, but it helps to know that Jesus walks with us through the pain—whether it be your death or a loved one's. What does it mean to walk as Jesus walked, as he approached death?

A prayer retreat: Luke 22:39–46

39 Jesus went out as usual to the Mount of Olives, and his disciples followed him.

Jesus left the city for a quiet, isolated place, where he could prepare for his imminent agony. It was a refuge, on a mountain, in nature, a familiar place, which he had frequented with his disciples. Get away to a favorite spot—a cabin in the mountains or a beach retreat. Get out of your routine and seek God. Prepare yourself spiritually.

40 On reaching the place, he said to them, "Pray that you will not fall into temptation." 41 He withdrew about a stone's throw beyond them, knelt down and prayed,

It is better not to go alone. When you are looking death in the face, you need people around you, but you choose how much time to spend with them. Jesus shared his heart with his disciples in a special time in the Upper Room (Jn. 13–16). If you are with someone who is dying, make sure they have the opportunity to be with the people most important to them. When my sister-in-law was dying, she wanted a cruise with friends and family around New York Bay. Unfortunately, it never happened, and she had to grab a few minutes with friends and family here and there. If you are the one approaching death, be sure to get that time. The movie "Get Low" is about a man who held his funeral before he died, and had a wonderful time with friends and family.

On the other hand, you can get too much of a good thing. A dying person tires easily and has lots to think about. At this point, your time alone with God is very important. Help your dying friend get that alone time. Try to "withdraw" as Jesus did, so you can commune with God; do not let that get crowded out. With all the doctors and visitors around, you may have to fight for it.

Wrestling with God's will

42 "Father, if you are willing, take this cup from me; yet not my will, but yours be done."

Talk honestly with the Lord. Jesus knew his Father's will, but in his humanity, like any man, he did not want to die. Nobody wants to suffer. It is always appropriate to ask for healing, for that bitter cup to be taken from you.

It will probably be a struggle, but it is important to reach that point of surrender. Trust in God; your life is in his hands, and he knows what he is doing. He will be with you in the valley of the shadow of death. At some point, we are all going to die. It is important to accept what God has planned for you and be at peace with it. If you are walking with someone facing death, give him the chance to talk, and encourage him to entrust himself totally to the Lord. Don't be afraid to talk with him about his fears and feelings regarding death. Eternity is at stake, and we want to do what we can to prepare him to meet his Lord. Don't be afraid to talk about his relationship to Christ and whether he is confident of his eternal salvation. It is terrible to regret lost opportunities once the person is gone, and think that you could have made the difference between them going to heaven or hell.

43 An angel from heaven appeared to him and strengthened him.

This is the fight of your life. It will drain all your strength. On your own, you cannot make it, but God will give you the strength to endure the pain and separation from your loved ones. You can ask for that same angel to strengthen you. God may use you to be that "angel"—ask him to help you minister strength to the one who is suffering.

44 And being in anguish, he prayed more earnestly, and his sweat was like drops of blood falling to the ground.

Even after submitting to his Father's will and receiving strength from the angel, Jesus continued to agonize in prayer. There will be discouraging and depressing days, even after accepting death and surrendering to God's will. In this case, Jesus sweated blood. His very life was being squeezed out of him in this great inner struggle. It is not easy. Never try to downplay the anguish of someone approaching death. Avoid super-spiritual talk: "Just trust in God. Where is your faith? Soon you will be in heaven!" Anguish is part of death.

Why are you sleeping?

45 When he rose from prayer and went back to the disciples, he found them asleep, exhausted from sorrow.46 "Why are you sleeping?" he asked them. "Get up and pray so that you will not fall into temptation."

Do not count on the support of family and friends. They are also sad, depressed, and angry—along with all kinds of other emotions. When you need them most, they may be caught up in their feelings and exhaustion, unable to provide the support you need. Only God will be your perfect companion on this hard road. At times, the person facing death ends up ministering to others!

If you find yourself in the position of the disciples, with someone in their final days, listen to the cry of their heart. If they ask you to pray, pray. If they want to be alone, leave them in peace. Do not be so self-centered that your grief robs them of the fellowship or prayer they long for.

The devil will always try to take advantage of our pain to tempt us, make us doubt God, or push us into sin. Stay strong spiritually so you do not fall into temptation. Only a few hours later, Peter would deny Jesus three times. He fell into that temptation. You may be tempted to distance yourself from the dying person, but that is when they most need your love. If you are dying, you may be tempted to doubt God's love or even his existence. Do not "fall asleep;" do what is necessary to stay alert spiritually, whether it be through prayer, recorded worship music, or the ministry of a pastor or brothers in Christ.

Help someone carry their cross: Luke 23:26–46

26 As the soldiers led him away, they seized Simon from Cyrene, who was on his way in from the country, and put the cross on him and made him carry it behind Jesus. 27 A large number of people followed him, including women who mourned and wailed for him.

Death is humiliating. You always managed to carry the cross that life gave you, but now your body is failing you. Jesus had already lost much blood and could no longer carry the cross—and he was a carpenter, used to carrying heavy wood. When death approaches, we lose control. We can no longer make our own decisions; a doctor or family member makes them for us. There was no way Jesus could escape his death sentence, even though he had it in his power to call down angels to deliver him. It is humiliating to see women wailing for you, suffering, as they see your pain.

The time will come when we have to say, "I cannot carry this cross any longer," and give it to another person who is willing to walk with us on this final stretch of the journey. Could you be a Simon of Cyrene? Is there someone you can help carry their cross?

28 Jesus turned and said to them, "Daughters of Jerusalem, do not weep for me; weep for yourselves and for your children. 29 For the time will come when you will say, 'Blessed are the childless women, the wombs that never bore and the breasts that never nursed!'30 Then

"'they will say to the mountains, "Fall on us!" and to the hills, "Cover us!"'

31 For if people do these things when the tree is green, what will happen when it is dry?"

If we have the hope of heaven, we can say as Jesus said: "Do not weep for me." The person who dies in Christ goes to paradise with the Lord; those left behind must deal with the loss. We are in the last days, and suffering and persecution will likely increase. It is important to keep the perspective Jesus had here, and even encourage those we will leave behind.

They don't know what they're doing

³² *Two other men, both criminals, were also led out with him to be executed.* ³³ *When they came to the place called the Skull, they crucified him there, along with the criminals—one on his right, the other on his left.*³⁴ *Jesus said, "Father, forgive them, for they do not know what they are doing."*

In this life, there will always be plenty of people to offend you, even in the last hours of your life, but they often do not know what they are doing and act in ignorance. Some are sincere; they may believe they are serving the Lord or the state. We need to avoid a persecution complex, which is all too common in the church.

Much grace is needed to forgive the person who is killing you. There are stories today of martyrs forgiving the person about to behead them. Several times, Jesus said that God will not forgive us if we do not forgive others (Matt. 6:14–15; 18:21–35). In the days before death, it is critical to examine your heart and see if there is someone you need to forgive. Try to contact them and make things right before you die. Hold onto that forgiving attitude right up to death, thanking God for the confidence that all your sins are forgiven. If you are caring for someone who is dying, gently help him search his heart and release anyone he needs to forgive.

James and John wanted to sit on Jesus' left and right—in his kingdom. Now, in his death, Jesus has criminals on his left and his right.

Death is humiliating

And they divided up his clothes by casting lots.

You can't take it with you. This robe was Jesus' only possession—and now he loses it. He was likely stark naked on that cross. It can hurt to see someone drive off in your beloved car or fight over a treasured possession. But in death, it is glaringly evident that material things are not that important. If you do not get too attached to them, it will be easier to let them go as death approaches. Jesus had glorious garments awaiting him in heaven, which Peter, James, and John got a glimpse of on the Mount of Transfiguration. That robe was only for his earthly life.

All those clothes and other goodies are not really yours. You can help a dying person lovingly dispose of his possessions. It is better than watching people cast lots for them or fight over them.

[35] *The people stood watching, and the rulers even sneered at him. They said, "He saved others; let him save himself if he is God's Messiah, the Chosen One."*

[36] *The soldiers also came up and mocked him. They offered him wine vinegar* [37] *and said, "If you are the king of the Jews, save yourself."*

[38] *There was a written notice above him, which read: this is the king of the jews.*

I have seen people suffering on their deathbed, with a crowd of family and friends watching them. They may just want to be alone at that moment. It is too easy for someone to sneer at them in their helplessness, talking about their past, their mistakes, and their weaknesses. Try to help a dying person maintain some dignity. Jesus could have said all kinds of things from the cross — or called down curses on them. He said nothing. The others had no idea what they were saying.

Today, you will be with me in paradise

[39] One of the criminals who hung there hurled insults at him: "Aren't you the Messiah? Save yourself and us!"

[40] But the other criminal rebuked him. "Don't you fear God," he said, "since you are under the same sentence? [41] We are punished justly, for we are getting what our deeds deserve. But this man has done nothing wrong."

[42] Then he said, "Jesus, remember me when you come into your kingdom."

[43] Jesus answered him, "Truly I tell you, today you will be with me in paradise."

This is the last chance for salvation. Once you are dead, there is no opportunity for repentance and forgiveness. There are some, like the first criminal, who only think about superficial things at that moment. Some people get angry at God and everyone else as they approach death. Instead of humbling themselves, they hold onto their pride. Interestingly, Jesus never responded to the first criminal. Maybe he knew it was too late at that point for him to repent and be saved.

Even with his dying breaths, Jesus was ministering to others and welcoming them into his kingdom. Wouldn't it be great to testify to God's goodness and draw others into the kingdom on our deathbeds!

It is finished

⁴⁴ It was now about noon, and darkness came over the whole land until three in the afternoon, ⁴⁵ for the sun stopped shining. And the curtain of the temple was torn in two.⁴⁶ Jesus called out with a loud voice, "Father, into your hands I commit my spirit." When he had said this, he breathed his last.

With his last words, Jesus committed himself to his Father. I have heard many stories of a dying person waiting to see a loved one; once that was taken care of, they let go and passed to the next life. It seems we have some control over that exact moment.

Death is cruel. Even the strongest believer can feel abandoned by God. It is fine to cry out to the Lord! Of course, this was the first time in all eternity that Jesus had been separated from his Father, as he bore the sins of all humanity, an overwhelming burden we cannot even begin to comprehend. In John's Gospel, Jesus says, *"It is finished."* He accomplished what he came for. His job—and his earthly life—was finished. How sad to see someone die with regrets of unfinished business and ruined relationships. Try to live life so you can say "It is finished," knowing you have done God's will and expect to hear, "Well done, good and faithful servant."

You do not know when you are going to die. Jesus knew how his life would end, but very few of us do. Sometimes death comes at an advanced age, sometimes after a lingering illness, where we are told how long we have. But too often, you hear of a man who leaves home in the morning, and an accident on the road claims his life. Or someone apparently in top condition suddenly dies of a heart attack. Or is murdered. Live as though this could be your last day. Keep short accounts with other people. Do not wait to get things right with God. Do what you can to make sure those you love will be provided for. Do not waste your time or your life;

make every moment count. Learn from Jesus how to approach death—your own or someone else's.

Conclusion: I Am With You Always

Matthew 28: 16–20

The disciples spent three years walking with Jesus, watching him, and learning to walk as he walked. Now it is time to put it all into practice and establish the church, the Body of Christ on earth. One of Jesus' last commands is a call for workers to go and make disciples. In this book, we have seen the possibility of actually completing what the disciples began in obedience to the Great Commission:

Then the eleven disciples went to Galilee, to the mountain where Jesus had told them to go. When they saw him, they worshiped him; but some doubted. Then Jesus came to them and said, "All authority in heaven and on earth has been given to me. Therefore go and make disciples of all nations, baptizing them in the name of the Father and of the Son and of the Holy Spirit, and teaching them to obey everything I have commanded you. And surely I am with you always, to the very end of the age" (Matt. 28: 16–20).

Even after three years of walking with the Son of God and being with the resurrected Lord, some doubted! Which are you? A worshiper? Or a doubter? To worship is more than singing praise songs; to worship is to serve and honor Jesus. After reading this book (and the first two in this series), it is time to put it into practice. If you want to walk like Jesus and be his disciple, here are seven points from his Great Commission to guide you:

1. The Father has given Jesus all authority, both here on earth and in heaven. Jesus shares his authority with you to heal, cast out demons, and preach the Word. If you choose to submit to his authority, it will flow through you and enable you to do his will.

2. Jesus told them to go; there is movement involved here. You may have to wait for the baptism of the Holy Spirit, as he commanded them in Acts 1, but if the message of this book has touched your heart, get ready to go under God's authority to reach many people, following the Master's Plan. In the first volume, you learned what it means to walk like Jesus, and in the second, you had the opportunity to immerse yourself in kingdom culture. Now you have seen the work God has for us in the kingdom; this is your chance to say to Jesus: "Here I am, send me."

3. Your main task is to make disciples. Not converts, but students committed to walk like Jesus walked.

4. It is missionary work; Jesus sends us to the nations. You may not go, but you should pray and support the worldwide work of the church.

5. The baptism of identification with Jesus Christ and union with him and his Father, and the filling of the Holy Spirit, should be integral parts of your ministry. Water baptism is for those who have made the decision to be Jesus' disciples and are willing to learn and obey his Word.

6. The Gospels will be central in your life and teaching. The goal is not impressive knowledge but impressive obedience. It cannot be selective; Jesus expects us to obey *everything* that he commanded us.

7. In all of this, he promises never to leave you. You will experience more of his presence when you are busy with what he told you to do.

How can he say that he would always be with them when he was about to ascend to his Father? How is he always with you? He shared the secret in the Upper Room the night of his arrest (Jn. 14:15–21):

"If you love me, keep my commands. And I will ask the Father, and he will give you another advocate to help you and be with you forever— the Spirit of truth. The world cannot accept him, because it neither sees him nor knows him. But you know him, for he lives with you and will be in you. I will not leave you as orphans; I will come to you. Before long, the world will not see me anymore, but you will see me. Because I live, you also will live. On that day you will realize that I am in my Father, and you are in me, and I am in you. Whoever has my commands and keeps them is the one who loves me. The one who loves me will be loved by my Father, and I too will love them and show myself to them."

Do you love Jesus? Are you just saying that, or are you ready to obey what he commands you to do in the Great Commission? The more you walk in that love and obedience, the more you will experience the love of God and the fullness of his Spirit.

Do you have limited resources? Is your church small? It does not matter! You do not need to do grand things or be part of a mega church. God will multiply the little you do and the little you have. The nature of the kingdom is of impressive growth, as we see in these parables:

Parable of the growing seed

He also said, "This is what the kingdom of God is like. A man scatters seed on the ground. Night and day, whether he sleeps or gets up, the seed sprouts and grows, though he does not know how. All by itself the soil produces grain—first the stalk, then the head, then the full kernel in the head. As soon as the grain is ripe, he puts the sickle to it, because the harvest has come" (Mark 4: 26-29).

An integral part of God's kingdom is spreading the seed of the Word. There are several phases in the growth of that seed, but God gives the growth until it is harvested. Are you scattering the seed of the Word? Are you surrounded by ripe grain? Do you know how to put the sickle to it? The harvest may be very close!

Parable of the mustard seed

Again he said, "What shall we say the kingdom of God is like, or what parable shall we use to describe it? It is like a mustard seed, which is the smallest of all seeds on earth. Yet when planted, it grows and becomes the largest of all garden plants, with such big branches that the birds can perch in its shade" (Mk. 4:30–32).

God's seed has been sown all over the world. God takes the smallest seed and makes it grow. Now we can expect an expansion, a multiplication, of everything that has been sown over the centuries. God wants his kingdom to become big and powerful, providing protection and shelter to multitudes.

Walking with Jesus in Acts

The apostles' experience is recorded in the book of Acts. Once again, Jesus gives them the promise of the Holy Spirit and his purpose:

On one occasion, while he was eating with them, he gave them this command: "Do not leave Jerusalem, but wait for the gift my Father promised, which you have heard me speak about. For John baptized with water, but in a few days you will be baptized with the Holy Spirit. You will receive power when the Holy Spirit comes on you; and you will be my witnesses in Jerusalem, and in all Judea and Samaria, and to the ends of the earth" (Acts 1:4, 5, 8).

The baptism in the Spirit is essential if we are to evangelize and make disciples of all nations. The last volume of this series will share how they continued to walk like Jesus and began to fulfill the Great Commission, with a miraculous multiplication of disciples. There have been many ups and downs in the history of the church: great revivals, and moments when we lose sight of this Great Commission. We are very close to Christ's return. This is a special moment to work with all our strength to fulfill his Great Commission.